LEGENDS OF THE
MAHASIDDHAS

LEGENDS OF THE
MAHASIDDHAS

Lives of the
Tantric Masters

TRANSLATED BY KEITH DOWMAN
ILLUSTRATED BY ROBERT BEER

Inner Traditions
Rochester, Vermont • Toronto, Canada

Inner Traditions
One Park Street
Rochester, Vermont 05767
www.InnerTraditions.com

Originally published in 1988 by Inner Traditions under the title *Masters of Enchantment: The Lives and Legends of the Mahasiddhas*
Second edition published in 1998 by Inner Traditions under the title *Buddhist Masters of Enchantment: The Lives and Legends of the Mahasiddhas*

Library of Congress Cataloging-in-Publication Data
Abhayadatta, author.
  [Caturasitisiddhapravrtti. English]
  Legends of the mahasiddhas : lives of the Tantric masters / translated by Keith Dowman ; illustrated by Robert Beer. — Third edition.
       pages cm
  Previously published as: Masters of enchantment, 1988 and Buddhist masters of enchantment, 1988.
    ISBN 978-1-62055-365-7 (paperback)
  1. Siddhas—Biography—Early works to 1800. 2. Tantric Buddhism—India—Early works to 1800. I. Dowman, Keith, translator. II. Beer, Robert, 1947– III. Title.
  BQ342.A2313 2014
  294.3'9250922—dc23
  [B]
                                                                            2014015356

Printed and bound in the United States by Versa Press, Inc.

10 9 8 7 6 5 4 3 2 1

Text design and layout by Virginia Scott Bowman
This book was typeset in Garamond Premier Pro

To send correspondence to the author or artist of this book, mail a first-class letter c/o Inner Traditions • Bear & Company, One Park Street, Rochester, VT 05767, and we will forward the communication, or contact the author directly at **www.keithdowman.net** or the artist directly at **www.tibetanart.com**.

CONTENTS

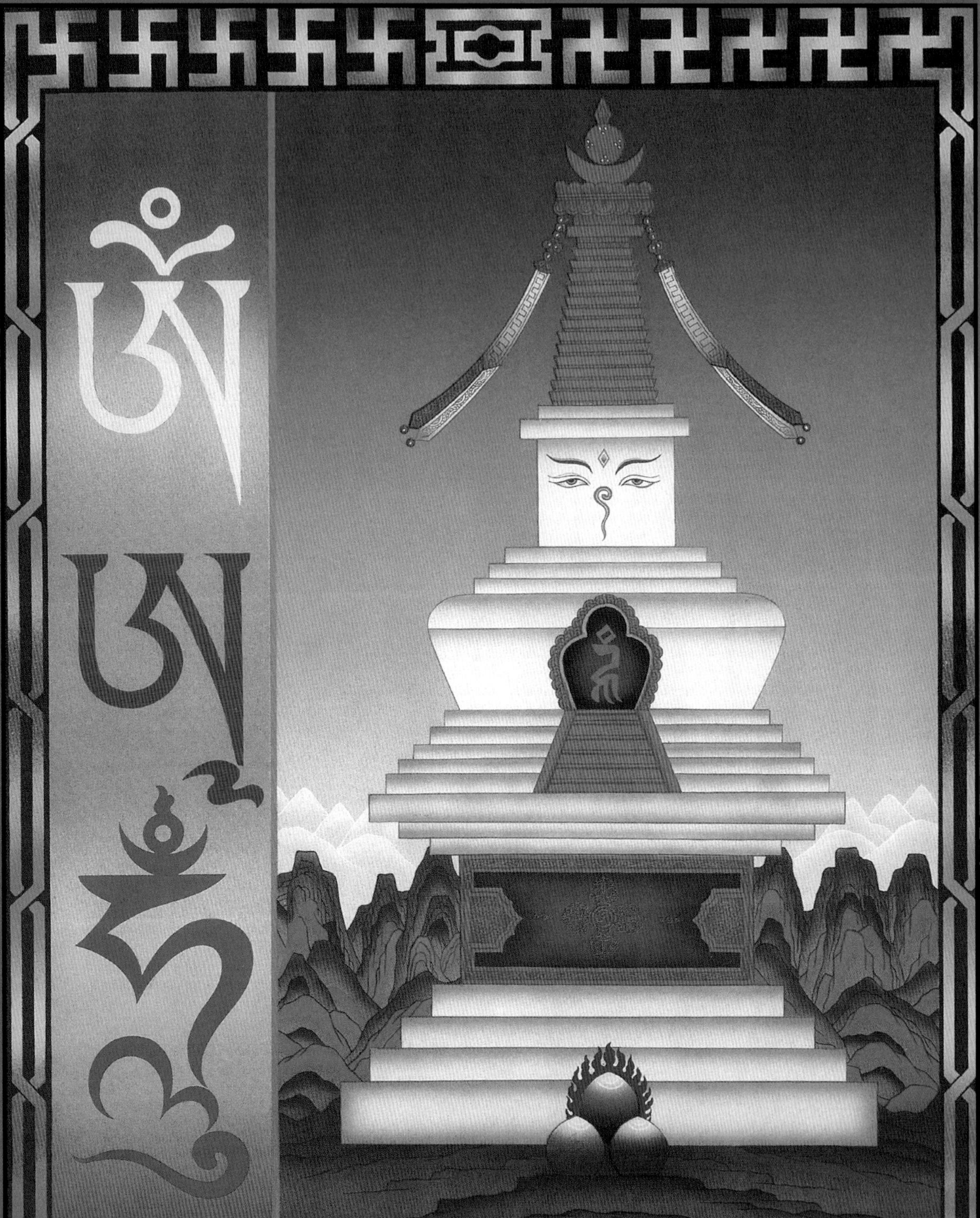
ཨོཾ
ཨཱ
ཧཱུྃ

AUTOBIOGRAPHICAL NOTE
By the Illustrator

Legends of the Mahasiddhas is the third edition of this book, which was first published in 1989 under the title of *Masters of Enchantment,* then again in 1998 as *Buddhist Masters of Enchantment.* For the second edition I wrote a short and now somewhat outdated biography, as the drawings and paintings I made for this book date back half of my lifetime to a ten-year period between 1977 and 1987.

In 1977 I was living in Bath, England, when Keith Dowman asked me to create a series of 84 individual drawings to illustrate the legends of the Eighty-four Buddhist Mahasiddhas of medieval India, which he had just finished translating from a woodblock-printed Tibetan text. Keith and I knew each other from the early seventies, when we both lived in India and Nepal. Keith was one of the first Western translators of Tibetan texts, while I was one of the first Western practitioners of Tibetan art and its iconography. Life was different back then. Photocopy machines weren't yet available in India, so everything had to be drawn by hand with a fine brush beneath the dim glow of a kerosene lamp, or tapped out on the faded ribbon of a portable typewriter, with a carbon-paper copy serving as a backup. Mistakes were easy to make but hard to correct, so patience, perseverance and dedication were our real teachers at this time.

After having made about thirty of these drawings for an agent who subsequently let us down, this project then came to the attention of the English illustrator Roger Dean, whose 1975 book, *Views,* distributed through Virgin Record stores, became a number one bestseller before even reaching a single UK bookshop. On the strength of this success Roger established the Dragon's World publishing company to showcase the work of some fine visionary artists of that time, and he proposed the production of an illustrated color book on the Mahasiddha legends. For a period of time Roger financed me to work on this project, during which I made about twenty Mahasiddha paintings, which appear in this book. But sadly, after a year or so, this project had to be curtailed. It then remained shelved for several years until Ehud Sperling, the president of Inner Traditions, recommissioned the book. So I started work on the illustrations once again in 1984 and made another set of drawings and ten new paintings.

The originals of these last ten paintings, which I painted between 1985 and 1987 while living in the Highlands of Scotland, are slightly larger and of a finer quality than the ones I made about seven years earlier. By this time I had learned a lot more about Tibetan iconography, had become far more patient and skillful at drawing with a fine brush and had developed my own techniques for using a Paasche AB Turbo Airbrush, which when mastered is a wonderful tool for working with gouache pigments. These ten later paintings are Luipa, Aryadeva, Nagarjuna, Naropa, Tilopa, Bhusuku, Jalandhara, Ghantapa, Carbaripa, and Udhilipa.

The drawings were all made with a brush and Chinese ink on hammered art paper, with each taking on average 24 hours to draw. Each gouache (opaque watercolor) painting took between 80 and 120 hours to paint, thus making a total of more than 4,000 hours to complete the artwork for this book. Although some purveyors of Oriental art claim that their artists use a single-hair brush or the "eyelash of a camel" for their fine detail work, this is not true, as many hairs are needed to hold the ink or pigments. The 000 size brush I used first had to be worn down to a fraction of its size for fine line work, while the control of one's breath always had to be regulated, especially for the drawing of long curving and tapering lines. In many ways the skill of line drawing like this with a brush is comparable to brain surgery.

I developed a keen interest in drawing at an early age and learned a lot about perspective and technical drawing from copying sketches in a 1940s book, *Tanks and How to Draw Them*. In retrospect the progression from drawing weapons of warfare to ferocious tantric deities makes some kind of sense in relation to the question I am most frequently asked, which is: "How did you first get involved with drawing and painting Tibetan deities?"

I was born with red-green colorblindness, so I couldn't get into art college. Disappointed at first, I came to realize this was a good thing, as I wasn't conditioned by modern conceptualism, much of which I still feel is anathema to the human soul. When I was thirteen my little sister died from hydrocephalus at the age of three, and her parting gift to me came in the form of a vivid dream, where in spirit we flew through a heavenly sky together and she was no longer a deformed child, but a highly intelligent and beautiful young girl. The reality of this "after-death communication" still remains crystal clear to me after more than fifty years. This innate experience of the human spirit's continuity marked the beginning of my spiritual journey, for I knew then what love and bereavement meant, but not why they are visited upon us, and the world of my childhood was never the same again.

Shortly after this my family broke up, and by the age of seventeen I had "dropped out" of everything and was living on the road, where I soon encountered the Gnostic traditions of the East, the symbolism of which profoundly inspired my artistic vision and creativity. Then in late 1968 I entered a psychedelically induced psychosis or "kundalini-crisis" that was to last for many years and change the course of my life. It was in this extremely volatile state of mental and perceptual distortion that I left for India and Nepal in 1970, where I was to live for nearly six years. And it was here that I became deeply involved in depicting the peaceful and wrathful visionary realms of Vajrayana Buddhist art. This wasn't really a philosophical or academic decision; it was intuitive, primordial, and aboriginal. The imagery closely mirrored my own inner process in an ever-deepening search for authentic meaning; art is outside, heart is inside.

The above is a short mythology of "how it all began," while the rest is essentially internal. I spent over twenty-five years at the drawing board, often working around the clock, and the many drawings and paintings I made during this time have appeared in several hundred books and are now widely pirated to adorn countless websites and spiritual artifacts. The main projects I have undertaken are a series of still unpublished Buddhist lineage holder drawings and *The Encyclopedia of Tibetan Symbols and Motifs* (1999), with its more concise offspring, *The Handbook of Tibetan Symbols* (2003), which are both published by Shambhala Publications.

I now live in Oxford, England, with my partner Gill, where I continue to research and write about Tibetan iconography, which I now know to be more than one lifetime's work. Over the past twenty years I have also been working with some of the finest Newar artists of the Kathmandu Valley, who paint both Hindu and Buddhist deities with incredible skill and dedication. Much of their work can now be viewed on my website: www.tibetanart.com.

ROBERT BEER,
FEBRUARY 2014

INTRODUCTION

Nothing can illuminate the nature of Tantric Buddhism better than the lives of the masters who founded it. In the vast corpus of Tibetan literature is a text called "The Legends of the Eighty-four Mahasiddhas." This unique collection of stories is believed to have been transmitted orally by an Indian scholar, Abhaya Datta Sri, to a Tibetan translator, Mondub Sherab, in the twelfth century, just before Buddhism in India disappeared. These legends portray the ethos of the Indian tantric tradition, the nature of the yogas and meditations of the tantric masters, and the mythological net that protects their secrets from uninitiated eyes.

However, in the transmission of the universal, practical elements of Tantric Buddhism from East to West, obscure and archaic Indian cultural content becomes an obstacle to understanding. Thus, while adapting the legends of the mahasiddhas from the literal Tibetan translation, our approach has been to stress in each legend the human qualities that transcend apparent cultural differences and to emphasize the principles of tantric practice. This involved the omission of duplication and irrelevancies, the elaboration of descriptive obscurities, and in a few legends even modification of the storyline. The number of legends has been reduced from eighty-four to fifty-four, but the meaning of the verse of instruction that enshrines the secret teaching of guru to disciple at the heart of each of these remaining stories has been rendered as closely as possible to the original Tibetan. In this way we hope to have eliminated the abstruse content of the legends, providing an accessible context for an understanding of the vital elements of the siddhas' philosophy of nonduality and emptiness.

THE SIDDHA TRADITION

It was the end of an era. The great achievements of the Gupta period had already become history in eighth century India, and there was a lull before the final blooming of Hindu civilization. Society had become obsessed with inflexible

1

rules and regulations. Just as form and procedure ruled society, stifling spirit and feeling, so ritual dominated religion. The pundits of the great academies devoted themselves to scholastic hairsplitting in a dead language, and sadhus sold their blessings in the marketplace. On India's western border the Turkish hordes were massing. The terrible threat of their invasion, with burning, pillaging, and massacre, was a sword of Damocles held over the Indian subcontinent.

In this environment a new form of Buddhism arose that was to regenerate a suffocating society. This third and final development of the Buddha Sakyamuni's teaching was called Tantric Buddhism, or Vajrayana. Tantra grew to dominate the religious life of India. It spread to Central Asia, China, and Japan, and it came to permeate every aspect of life in Tibet. Until recently Western scholars have taken an orthodox Brahmin view of heterodox Tantra, or they have perceived it from the earlier hinayana or mahayana Buddhist perspectives. But in the last twenty years Tibetan lamas in exile from their homeland have demonstrated a pure, living tantric tradition to the West, and this has forced a reappraisal of Tantra.

The exemplars of the new Buddhism, the high priests of Tantra, were called siddhas. In the beginning, in eighth century India, they represented a pure and purifying spirituality arising from the grass roots of society. Alienated from the dead forms of the social and religious establishment, equating society with life's confusion, renunciation was a prerequisite to spiritual attainment. The ethos of their pure mysticism made them antiestablishment, unorthodox, and antischolastic. They stressed the simple and free life rather than institutional discipline. Militating against empty ritual, charlatanism, specious philosophizing, the caste system, and Brahminical ritual purity, they were iconoclastic rebels. They taught existential involvement rather than metaphysical speculation. Many siddhas were musicians and poets who sang their realization in wonderful mystical songs in vernacular languages, using metaphors of home and family, farming and crafts, love and sex.

The siddhas were never to compromise their radical attitudes to orthodoxy, and they maintained their ideal of existential freedom at all cost. But as Tantra became more widely accepted its proponents became identified less and less with the itinerant yogin belonging to a secret outcaste cult. From the ninth to the twelfth centuries eastern India was dominated by an empire ruled by a Buddhist dynasty who patronized tantric Buddhism. Under the Pala kings the tantric revolution became accepted by the establishment. Although institutionalism and Tantra remained inimical, the Pala kings established monastic academies, like Vikramasila and Oddantapuri, where tantric literature was studied and a vast body of commentary on the basic tantric texts written down.

In this later evolution of Tantric Buddhism the profound tolerance and breadth of vision of the siddhas was shown by their thorough permeation of society. The eighty-four mahasiddhas came from every walk of life and represented an entire spectrum of human experience. They were Brahmin priests and scholars, monks and nuns, kings and ministers, merchants and shopkeepers, hunters and servants. Counted amongst the greatest of the siddhas is a washerman, a cowboy, a thief, a conman, a gambler, and a whore. Several siddhas suffered from serious diseases. The realization that embraced all men and women in the tantric fold—whatever their social status and mode of life—was an awareness of the Buddha nature in all sentient beings. The karma that bound them to tantric yoga was their meeting with a master, their initiation into a lineage of tantric instruction, and their practice of tantric meditation.

Although the Pala empire centered on Bengal became the powerhouse of Tantra, there were other areas of India that were of vital importance to the siddha tradition. Oddiyana in the northwest (the Swat Valley, now in Pakistan) originated several important tantric lineages. In the south of India, which may have been the area where the first tantric cults were established, Kanchi (Concheeveram in Tamil Nadu) was a major center of Tantric Buddhism. Also, the holy mountain of Sri Parbat (in Andhra Pradesh), mentioned several times in these legends, was established as a major tantric power place during the siddha period, a status it has retained until today. However, forty-seven of the eighty-four mahasiddhas were associated with eastern India, compared to nine with the south and only two with the northwest.

In the middle of the twelfth century the Buddhist Pala empire was defeated by the short-lived Hindu Sena dynasty. In 1199, during the invading Turks' final push against eastern India, a general mistook the academy of Vikramasila for a fort, massacred the monks, burnt the invaluable library, and destroyed the academy. In the rabid Muslim aftermath, in the absence of any patronage, deprived of both secular and temporal support, Buddhists throughout northern India died for their beliefs, accepted Islam rather than the sword, or fled into exile in the Himalayas. The tantric tradition in Nepal and Tibet benefited greatly from the influx of refugees from India. Thereafter, in its homeland, Buddhism went underground, finally to be absorbed by the more resilient Hindu tantric lineages. Elements of Buddhist Tantra can still be seen in the tradition of the Nath yogins, in the Sufi tradition of the great medieval mystic poet Kabir, and even in the modern Bengali poet Rabindranath Tagore.

DEFINING OUR TERMS

Who were these spiritual adventurers? What did they teach? What was their practice? In answering these questions it would be useful to define several Sanskrit words that remain untranslated throughout this work because they have no English equivalents.

The first is the word "siddha." Siddhas are practitioners of Tantra who are successful in attaining the goal of their meditation. This achievement is known as *siddhi*. It is twofold in that it confers both magical power (mundane) and enlightenment itself (supreme). The word "siddha" could be rendered "saint," "magus," "magician," or "adept." But even this is not sufficient, because "siddha" evokes an entire lifestyle, a unique mode of being, and a very particular form of aspiration. For uninitiated Indians the emphasis of their associations with siddhas is on magical power. If a yogin or yogini can walk through walls, fly in the sky, heal the sick, turn water into wine, levitate, or read minds, he or she may gain the title "siddha." If those same practitioners have a crazy glint in their eyes, cover themselves in ashes, bring tears to the eyes with their songs, calm street mongrels by their very presence, induce faithful women to leave their families, wear *vajras* in their yard-long hair knots, eat out of skull bowls, talk with the birds, cry when they see a spastic child, sleep with lepers, fearlessly upbraid powerful officials for moral laxity, or perform with conviction any act contrary to convention while demonstrating a "higher" reality, then they are doubly siddhas.

However, these are the popular notions of people who have no conception of the siddhas's spiritual and existential goal of *mahamudra,* which is Buddhahood. Of course, siddhas are also found working inconspicuously in offices, on farms, and in factories. A siddha may be a king, a monk, a servant, or a whore. The prefix "maha" means "great," "sublime," or "magnificent"; thus, the mahasiddhas are the greatest of the most accomplished of the siddhas.

The word *sadhana* has sometimes been translated "spiritual discipline." However, it also means "psycho-experimental techniques of personality transcendence and ecstasy," or "the activity of an integrated body, speech, and mind motivated by the Bodhisattva Vow." More specifically, sadhana is the yogin's or yogini's practice of the guru's meditation instruction, or an initiate's principal meditation liturgy.

Obviously, sadhana is a central concept in the life of a *tantrika* (a practitioner of Tantra). Sadhana becomes one's whole life. In fact, the degree to which one's life is not integrated into sadhana is the degree to which the pledge sworn at the time of initiation is broken. This pledge is the vow to selflessly devote one's entire being to the nondual, gnostic experience of enlightenment. The forms of the mahasiddhas' sadhanas are as varied as their personalities, although in the limited sense most of their meditation techniques belong to what is known as the creative and fulfillment modes of meditation.

The invariable goal of the siddhas' sadhanas is *mahamudra-siddhi,* which is nothing less than the enlightenment experienced by the Buddha himself. The easiest way of dealing with the vague and overworked term "enlightenment" is to define it as the attainment of a sustained ultimate experience of the oneness of all things, nondual cognition of ultimate reality, clear light, gnostic awareness, the dissolution of the individuated personality into the universal mind. The Buddha's enlightenment is specifically defined as coincident with that vast, empathetic, self-sacrificial social sensibility we call love. That is mahamudra-siddhi.

Mahamudra-siddhi is invariably accompanied by mundane siddhi, although not the reverse; and mundane siddhi is conventionally defined as attainment of the Eight Great Siddhis (Powers), the six extrasensory powers, and the four transformative modes of action.

The eight great powers are enumerated differently in the various traditions. The siddhis that Nagabodhi attained from Nagarjuna in these legends were the power to walk through matter; the power to wield the enchanted sword of wisdom; the power of annihilation and creation (materialization and dematerialization); the power of third-eye vision; the power to locate both physical and metaphysical treasures; the power of speed-walking; and the power to synthesize the pill of immortality. The language of this list may be interpreted literally or figuratively, according to the faith and understanding of the student. Thus, the power to walk through walls can be explained literally as a siddha's magical feat to induce faith in the credulous, or figuratively to demonstrate the nature of reality as a dream, an illusion, a hallucination, where all things are experienced as light and space.

All these siddhis must be understood in the light of the basic precept "all is mind." For the siddha there is no body-mind, body-spirit duality. What makes these siddhis "great" is their inherent capacity to be used as technical aids in sadhana.

The six extrasensory powers are mental powers of the same order as the great siddhis couched in psychic terminology: thought reading; memory of past lives; clairaudience ("the divine ear"—understanding of all languages, including those of animals and birds); clairvoyance ("the divine eye"—astral vision, especially intuition of another's suffering); ability to perform miracles (manipulation of the elements, flight, walking on water); and the ability to arrest and extinguish emotivity. These are all powers that the mahasiddha, who is a Bodhisattva, can employ to expedite the zero experience of ecstasy for themselves or others. The ability to evoke such powers at will outside meditation practice is a true sign of success in sadhana.

The transformative modes of action—pacification, enrichment, control, and destruction—include the eight great siddhis and the six types of extrasensory perception and all other skillful means that calm the mind, endow it with enriching qualities, control and manipulate it for any given purpose, or eliminate it. Although the means of effecting these four techniques of altering consciousness are a siddha's spontaneous accomplishment, the siddha remains impotent unless he or she has an immediate intuitive flash about what needs to be done. In that intuitive awareness—represented by four *dakinis*—lies the essential key to these four modes of action.

Another term we use frequently is *samsara*. Although there are several succinct phrases by which it can be rendered—"wheel of life," "round of rebirth," "cycle of confusion," "transmigratory existence"—all are poor translations. Exoterically, samsara is the frustrating cycle of rebirth through the human realm, heaven and hell, and the animal and spirit realms, destined by karma. Esoterically, samsara is the whirligig of mind toned by successive varied and complex emotional states described in terms of the penetrating psychology of the six realms and conditioned by thought.

In psychological terms, samsara is "anxiety," which all of us experience to some degree. However, in Western culture only acute anxiety is recognized as a state of mind that should be treated by a psychiatrist or minister. Psychosis, paranoia, delusions of grandeur, schizophrenia, and neurosis are all terms germane to descriptions of the realms of samsara. In Buddhist thought, all humanity is to some degree psychotic, or at best alienated, until release is attained. Whether viewed in terms of transmigration, the unsatisfactory human condition, anxiety, or neurosis, samsara is what all human beings sometimes, and some human beings always, wish to escape. Buddhism is primarily concerned with techniques that allow one to escape from samsara into nirvana. Where the word "release" or "liberation" is used in a Buddhist context, it always refers to release from samsara. The siddhas developed their own methods of release, which can be characterized as quick, democratic, demanding, and often dangerous.

The literal meaning of the word "Tantra" is rarely implied in common usage. It means "thread," "continuity," or "warp and woof." It refers to the one essential, immutable, and continuous element in life—emptiness or "suchness," the ultimate, indeterminate, existential reality inherent in ordinary consciousness. We use "Tantra" to indicate the ethos of a way of life determined by a body of practices described in a canon of texts, which themselves are called tantras.

Since only the self-evident and sensational elements of Tantra—ritualism, sex, and magic—are widely known, the common associations of the term are unbalanced and misleading. Of the four classes of Buddhist Tantra (we will not discuss the similar but different Hindu Tantra), the lower levels are predominantly ritualistic and to a larger extent concerned with attainment of temporal goals and magical powers. The higher levels of Tantra do involve ritual meditation, but in the supreme Tantra (*anuttara-yoga* Tantra), which leads to mahamudra-siddhi, ritualism *per se* is rejected. The eighty-four paradigms of tantric practice given in these legends describe nonritualistic meditation. Although sex is abhorred in orthodox Buddhism, in Tantra it is accepted as a valid means by which mahamudra can be attained. The mistaken notion that tantric yoga is sexual yoga is fostered by the tantras' frequent use of sexual analogies, metaphors, and symbols to describe psychic processes.

A LOOK AT THE TANTRAS

To understand the metaphysical content of the siddhas' teaching it is useful to look at tantric literature. These texts are based upon what are known as the "root tantras." Each text deals with the practice associated with a particular deity. Thus, each of the deities Guhyasamaja, Cakrasamavara, Hevajra,

Mahamaya, and Yamari—the most important of the deities associated with the siddhas—has a root tantra that describes his mandala in terms of his divine entourage (an assemblage of spiritual forces); the creative and fulfillment modes of meditation; subsidiary rites (fire sacrifice, extensive feasts and offerings); detailed descriptions of symbology and of ingredients for symbolic offerings; and other sections specific to the individual tantra. For example, the Hevajra-tantra includes a section on the psychological effects of different gazes.

It is certain that the tantras were being transmitted orally for hundreds of years before they began to be written down in their literary form in the fifth century AD. However, we can only speculate about who practiced these rites and who formed the early lineages. Most probably Tantra was the preserve of outcastes transmitting a system of ritual magic associated with their fertility goddesses, a tradition that may have had its roots in pre-Aryan India. Only much later would they have assimilated the Brahmin's vedic gods, elements of Patanjali's yoga, and finally a soteriological system defining a method of liberation from samsara along with meditation techniques.

When we strip away the ritual content of the root tantras, what remains is a very small but all-important body of metaphysical lore at the center of which lies the concept of the "Absolute"—the dynamo that gave the siddhas their enormous spiritual energy, power, and realization and charged them with their amazing self-confidence and drive. However, the siddhas constantly claimed that they had no concept of the Absolute, not even any knowledge of the Absolute. For, by its very nature, the Absolute is beyond thought, and thus beyond the capacity of temporal mind to comprehend. It is indefinable, indeterminable, without location.

One important term they used, and there were many, was "reality" (*tattva*, or in Tibetan [T.], *de-nyid*), or "suchness," "isness," and also "the absolute specific," for paradox is the most apposite manner of expressing it. The absolute specific of a single experience—as well of the entire space-time continuum—is emptiness (*sunyata*, T. *stong-pa-nyid*) and clear light (T. *od-gsal*). It has no origin and no root, and it is therefore termed "unborn" or "uncreated." It is the cosmic totality, and it is a grain of sand. Nevertheless, because reality is utterly indeterminable, there is no truth in any concept of truth, except that such concepts can lead to a progressive reduction in the process of conceptual thinking until finally it can be abandoned altogether.

THOUGHT AND PARADOX

Contempt for conceptual thought permeates Tantra. In the canonical tantras there is very little regard for logical consistency, and paradox appears constantly. The most beautiful paradox of all lies in the answer to a conceptual problem that is bound to arise when reading the siddhas' songs. Question: "If all things are absolute reality, emptiness, spaciousness, then what is the status of material form for the enlightened siddha?" Answer: "Emptiness is form and form is emptiness."

Emptiness is nothing if not form, and form does not disappear when all things are seen as spaciousness, for that would imply a contradiction to the constantly emphasized premise in mahayana Buddhism that there is no transcendental entity, or nonentity, outside the sensual realm, the realm of ordinary consciousness. To say that all things are conceived of as emptiness does not imply that the visual sense ceases to function. Rather, it implies that the noetic spaciousness of the perceiver coincides with the inherent spaciousness of the perceived. All phenomenal appearances are like the transparent skin of an egg, or better still, like a hologram where the knower and the known, "self" and "other," become unified. This leads to the great mystery of mahamudra. This mystery can be conceived as a two-in-one union (*yuganaddha*) where both unity and duality become one simultaneous and continuous peak experience. The sexual analogy of lovers achieving a sense of complete oneness while still in their individual bodies is probably the best if not the only image we have that can express this paradoxical mystery.

Attainment of this union of self and other in mahamudra means eliminating the barriers between oneself and other people. Suddenly the social field opens up as the siddha empathizes totally with all sentient beings. With the powers of mind reading and prescience (the direct result of uniting self and other), the siddha is now capable of guiding others in sadhana.

Coincident with the attainment of the ultimate mystical experience, one is also imbued with compassion, which means, literally, "suffering together" and automatically fulfills the Bodhisattva Vow, which is the commitment to serve others without prejudice in whatever way is necessary. Loving-kindness, sympathetic joy, compassion, and equanimity—the four boundless states of mind—constitute a preparatory meditation that cultivates the feeling of oneness with all beings. In a perfect dance of reciprocity, the mahamudra union generates these social virtues and, in turn, these feelings induce that union.

The siddhas of the legends were renowned for their spontaneous outpourings of feeling, whether it was for a starving puppy or the beauty of a woman. The songs (caryagiti) of the siddhacaryas are full of profound sentiments of love for woman.

SKILLFUL MEANS AND PERFECT INSIGHT

The dual elements of the mahamudra union are skillful means and perfect insight (*upaya,* T. *thabs* and *prajna,* T. *shes-rab*), the first being the male coordinate and the second the female. The guru embodies the skillful means necessary to achieve the pure pleasure of enlightenment, and the dakini brings the perfect insight and wisdom—the union of pure awareness and ecstasy. Contrary to Hindu Tantra, in Buddhist Tantra these poles are not characterized as passive and active. Rather, stasis lies in separation and alienation (failure to recognize union), while dynamic energy is the result of union. The two basic dualistic terms are interpreted differently in different sadhanas, as well as at different levels of progress and for different ends.

In general, however, skillful means is designated as compassion, and perfect insight as emptiness. Given this context, compassion is not to be defined as pity or even as divine love. Compassion here is the Bodhisattva's sensibility responding spontaneously to the demands of the outer world with an immense variety of skillful means at hand.

These means are expressed by the entire pantheon of tantric deities, particularly the wrathful deities that represent conformations of the psychic forces that transmute negative energies into the elixir of pure pleasure. The faces of these deities are represented as masks in the Tibetan tankas (painted scrolls) to indicate that there is no attachment to the violent emotions the faces depict. For example, acting out of compassion, the vajrasiddha may emanate a fierce form of anger to destroy fear in another, while remaining invulnerable to that emotion through detachment.

The coordinate of male compassion is female emptiness. The complete definition of perfect insight is "penetrating insight into the nature of all things as emptiness." Thus, perfect insight and emptiness become similar aspects of the one indeterminate absolute, pure nondual awareness. Whenever compassion and emptiness unite, it is rendered self-aware, empty, and absolutely specific. This is the dakini's blessing.

PURE PLEASURE

The siddhas enjoyed their sadhana. The psychological types who needed a simple life took to the road rather than practicing the radical asceticism that led some of their contemporaries to torment their bodies or minds in destructive self-abnegation (*tapas*). The siddhas practiced purification, of course. But for them, guilt was eradicated by initiation. Sin was seen only as the failure to practice meditation and any tendency to take an extreme view.

They saw life as an audiovisual spectacular, a dance of ephemeral energy configurations that some called Mahamaya, the female personification of "magnificent illusion." "Live as a child lives," they taught. "The world is full of natural happiness. Dance, sing, and enjoy it! Enjoy the pleasures of your senses, but"—and here was the element that distinguished the siddha from the neurotic sensualist—"don't be attached to them. Draw water, but don't get wet!"

Thus, enjoyment was both the result of sadhana and also the means for attaining it. Among the eighty-four siddhas there were many individuals whose object of meditation was sensually delightful—flowers, birdsong, music, and also sexual intercourse. The result of sadhana is "pure" pleasure (*mahasukha,* T. *bde-ba-chen*), which is qualitatively different from the heightened sensations of sensual experience. Pure pleasure is the feeling tone of the Buddha's mode of being as empty space, and it is essential to grasp the nature of this ultimate plane of being and relate it to the relative planes.

Emptiness, the *dharmakaya* (T. *chos-sku*), the ultimate existential mode of experience is all-inclusive. The words that characterize it are expressive of the inexpressible, an inconceivable non-duality, pure awareness, emptiness, pure pleasure, all-pervasive space (*dhatu,* T. *dbyings*), and clear light. The relative modes of visionary enjoyment, the *sambhogakaya* (T. *longs-spyod-sku*) and apparitional incarnation, the *nirmanakaya* (T. *sprul-sku*), are the duality that unites as the ultimate mahamudra mode.

The male coordinate of skillful means corresponds to the mode of visionary enjoyment and discriminating aesthetic delight where guidance is found in the form of ubiquitous divine archetypes and symbolic indications. The essential nature of this mode of being is radiant light.

The female coordinate of perfect insight corresponds to the mode of apparitional incarnation in which the dakini dances her magical display with tantalizing brilliance. In her essential nature she is manifest compassion.

These three modes may also be visualized as interpenetrating spheres, or as the center, radius, and circumference of a mandala. That is the doctrine of the Buddha's three modes of being (*trikaya*, T. *sku gsum*), and it is essential to an understanding of the siddhas's metaphysics.

THE GURU

The structural pattern of the legends is diagnosis, prescription, and cure. In these tales we find sick people aware of their sickness, and disgusted with their current lives. They are contrite and willing to do whatever is necessary to affect a cure. A guru inevitably appears, and after the disciple requests instruction, the guru grants initiation and offers precepts. These precepts are usually given in terms of instruction in the creative and fulfillment modes of meditation. The disciple performs this sadhana, attains mahamudra-siddhi and in the process is cured of the original disease. *Siddhas* attain Buddhahood in their lifetimes, and in their own bodies are assumed into the Paradise of the Dakinis.

Without exception, the legends stress the importance of the guru. This teacher must not be viewed simply as an extraordinary human being with certain special knowledge that can be transmitted, although this will be the preconception of the supplicant. And it is essential that the disciple approach the guru as a supplicant since, in the terms of the tantric commitment, the guru can only give precepts to those who approach with respect and request initiation and instruction at a propitious moment and an appropriate juncture.

However, initiation radically alters the guru-disciple relationship, destroying all the initiate's preconceptions. The heart of the initiation comes when the guru reveals himself as the Buddha, and the initiate identifies with this guru—Buddha. Thereafter, the initiate's basic practice is to be able to reproduce the ultimate experience of oneness and to assimilate it fully into everyday life. When the disciple can identify with all human beings and all appearances whatsoever, and his speech with all human speech and all sound whatsoever, and his mind with all-pervasive, pure, nondual awareness, he effectively identifies with the guru. Thus, although initiates will always retain respect for the human individual in whom the Buddha manifested at their initiation, their notion of the guru gradually expands to include all beings without exception, including themselves. Siddhas are beings who have this vision.

Many siddhas had incarnate dakini gurus. Many more had no human guru at all. Sometimes a wisdom dakini (T. *ye-shes mkha'-'gro*) appears in the realm of visionary enjoyment (sambhogakaya) to initiate a yogin at the propitious moment. If his capacity for creative imagination is sufficiently developed, he sees her in a vision before him; otherwise he may hear a voice or simply see her and hear her in his mind's eye—the result is the same. Sometimes the dakini takes human form. The mundane or worldly dakini (*jig-rten mkha'-'gro*) often appears as a whore or a dancing girl to the itinerant yogin.

Identification of "woman" with the dakini stresses the thoroughgoing nonduality of Tantra—every woman is the dakini. Even though she may lack experiential recognition of this, she is still the tantrika's dakini. For one siddha the dakini was his mother, and for another she was a young girl. The dakini guru is clearly most capable of empowering a yogin to practice the fulfillment mode of meditation by uniting with him as insight to his skillful means, and this happens frequently. Other siddhas have been initiated by Bodhisattvas—in particular, Manjusri, Lokesvara, and Tara—some appearing in divine form in the sphere of visionary enjoyment (sambhogakaya), while others incarnate (in nirmankaya).

THE CREMATION GROUND

Frequently in the legends gurus meet their disciples in a cremation ground. Cremation grounds are replete with all kinds of symbolic meaning. First, it is the deathbed of the ego. It is the obvious place to meet one's guru. The tantric yogin celebrates the cremation ground as an ideal place to meditate upon the precious human body, the transitory nature of existence, upon death and karmic retribution, and upon emptiness itself. It is also a good place to keep warm on bitter winter nights.

Thus, guru and disciple meet in empathy. And here the initiate dies to the world of confusion and is reborn into the world of light. Jackals and hyenas lurk in the shadows, shrieking and howling; crows and vultures wheel overhead, hoping as do the jackals to taste human flesh. While the funeral pyres crackle and the sparks fly upward, the dakini in the gut *cakra* ignites and melts concrete thought patterns. All the rigidity of the head center melts into the elixir of immortality and drips down into the dakini's skull cup. All phenomenal appearances take on an ethereal radiance. Sentient beings seem like apparitional phantoms in ecstasies of delight in the sepulchral fairyland.

Furthermore, it is here in the cremation ground that the initiate can find the appurtenances needed by the yogin—the skull cup, a human femur for a thigh-bone trumpet, other bones to carve into coronets, bracelets, and belts—for as bones are the substructure of the human body, so emptiness pervades reality.

INITIATION AND INSTRUCTION

It is clear that initiation is not merely a formal rite to show disciples where they are heading and to welcome them into the club. The initiation, which is also an empowerment, must also reveal the Buddha nature, the nature of mind, the indeterminate absolute, while the specific qualities of the deity into whose mandala the initiate is led must also be disclosed. This implies an extremely receptive, sensitive recipient, and a very perspicacious, powerful, and fully aware transmitter.

Most of the siddhas who had no previous meditation experience before they met their gurus were in the throes of acute loss, a spiritual vacuum brought about by extreme mental or physical pain, and were thus ripe for a radical change in mind (*metanoia*). At the bottom of the pit of samsaric suffering there is a point where one recognizes that one's own limitations and delusions had been such an integral part of the mind they could not be looked at objectively.

Along with this humbling recognition comes a new sense of fresh potential and high expectation of the precious human body. Thus, a rebound out of the pit may be incipient in hell itself. It is the guru's function to deflect the rebound away from the trap of rebirth into another realm, to direct it off the wheel of life altogether. In *The Tibetan Book of the Dead* such "traps" are described as different-colored lights that appear on the journey between death and rebirth and attract the consciousness of beings, according to their propensities.

Remorse and contrition are essential elements leading up to the desire for and the guru's decision to give initiation, much as in the Christian experience of "meeting Christ" and being "born again." The greater the sense of revulsion, shame, self-hatred, and nihilistic distress, the more receptive the initiate, and the more radical the "turning around in the seat of consciousness." Gurus must always arrive on the scene at the propitious moment, and if they are indeed *the* guru they always do.

After initiation comes instruction, which may have only a tenuous connection to the specific content of the initiation. However, the guru's instruction is more than the conveyance of concepts to be put into practice. In the first flush of the mystical experience of initiation, the guru/Buddha's word is essentially empty sound and pure pleasure. The pure awareness involved in this experience constitutes the most important aspect of the "secret teaching" (T. *man-ngag*).

Next, when the initiate listens to the guru's instruction with an open mind, symbolic overtones can usually be heard. This level of guidance, which transcends concepts, is direct and penetrating. The danger here lies in filtering these symbolic indications through a deluded mind, rather than intuitively permitting them to be assimilated instantly.

Lastly, the precepts enshrining the specific instruction on meditation are then to be practiced as sadhana. Most of the siddhas' practices fall into the creative and fulfillment modes. However, one of the definitions of Tantra is "the path of multiple means"—and this phrase contains an ocean of possibilities.

Interpreting "multiple means" broadly, Tantra or *vajrayana*—the path of practice taking the vajra (thunderbolt) as the symbol of ultimate, empty reality—includes within it the hinayana (lesser path) Buddhist practices of one-pointed concentration (*samatha*); guarding the doors of the senses (*vipasyana*); and strict personal discipline. And it also includes such mahayana (Bodhisattva's path) practices as meditation on emptiness; contemplation of the four boundless states of mind; and arousal of the *bodhicitta* of compassion. To these are added a vast variety of purely tantric practices such as visualization of deities; recitation of mantras, physical yoga, and manipulation of *prana* (breath); complex alchemical rites; formless meditation; and pilgrimages.

Tantra is also the path of multiple means because it employs the entire gamut of human activity as the basis of meditation, as the siddhas' sadhanas demonstrate: The king meditates on his throne; the farmer in his fields; the lecher in bed; and the widower on the cremation ground. Further, the yogin who sits in contemplation may be confronted by the most horrible neurotic confusion and startlingly perverse concepts. Any and every state of mind is the means to its own transformation. This means that the infinite variety of imperfect human personalities is also the multiplicity of means to attain mahamudra-siddhi.

ALCHEMY AND MEDITATION

The yogin is an alchemist who must transmute the base metal of a confused mind into the gold of pure awareness. The quality of the base metal in the yogin's possession is irrelevant. The philosopher's stone that turns everything to gold is actually a homeopathic dose of the poison that caused the yogin's original confusion.

If lust is the dominant mind poison, then meditation upon a controlled shot of desire—in the light of the guru's initiation and instruction—shows the disciple the emptiness of all desire. In the dawning realization of the ultimate nature of part of the mind comes the realization of the ultimate nature of the entire universe—this leads to mahamudra-siddhi.

The remedy for the original distress lies in the nature of the neurotic personality itself. The principle behind the cure is "like cures like," the axiom of homeopathy. The use of this innovative and highly risky technique is justified by the Buddha's prophecy that his doctrine would endure for five hundred years in its pure form and five hundred years in a modified form. Thereafter, in the *kaliyuga,* the age of strife, people would be unable to follow the discipline or find the compassion to practice the way of the hinayana *arhat* or the mahayana Bodhisattva. Then the way of the siddha would be revealed.

The sign of our being in the kaliyuga is the impatience of the disciple. Unwilling to live through eons of successive rebirths before attaining nirvana, the yogin wants results immediately. What takes the most time in Tantra is the process of purifying the mind, eradicating vice and passion, and cultivating virtue and clarity. One of the basic principles of Tantra is that good and evil, virtue and vice, and pleasure and pain are equally delusive. What is the use of clinging to the good and pleasant and rejecting the vicious and ugly when everything is of equal value as raw material in the process of transmutation?

The danger here is that the initiate can abuse this precept. However, the mistaken notion that vice and passion have the same ultimate quality as virtue and clarity is removed by the initiate's sworn obedience to the guru and by the commitments made at initiation. These commitments are called *samayas,* and if initiates break them they feel themselves in hell. The dangers of the tantric path are justified by the proven efficacy of tantric techniques. Proof enough is the continued existence of a pure lineage that is today still transmitting the precepts that transform ordinary consciousness into a siddha's awareness.

In alchemical meditation (*rasayana,* T. *bcud-len*) the obstacles met in other systems of meditation are here treated as friendly helpers on the path. Neurotic attitudes and environmental frustrations are the means of transcending such conditions. Lusts, attachments, deceits, fascinations, and fixations are the meat of meditation. Uninvited guests, an inopportune impingement of sound, paranoid delusions, and mental chatter all assist the yogin in becoming a siddha.

Nevertheless, it must be remembered that those siddhas who achieved the most renown and who initiated lineages that are still alive today in Tibetan practice—Luipa, Saraha, Tilopa, Naropa, Virupa, and Nagarjuna—were renunciate yogins who abandoned home and family ties, palaces and academies, security and comfort, fame and wealth, to practice their sadhanas in conditions of deprivation. Although they performed the same alchemical meditations, they first removed the principal causes of gross and acute fascination and attachment—the strongest agencies of the mind's structuring and conditioning.

CREATIVE MEDITATION

In creative meditation (*utpattikrama,* T. *bskyed-rim*) the yogin begins by identifying with the field of emptiness. Out of emptiness arises a seed syllable that is the quintessential euphonic corollary of the form of the principal deity of the mandala that is to be created. Employing the faculty of creative imagination, from this seed syllable arise the deity and his entourage of divine beings and consorts within a palace surrounded by walls with gates. Then the deities of the mandala are brought to life through mudra, symbolic gestures of the hands; mantra, recitation of the seed sounds of the deity; and visualization of the deities' forms.

In a *samadhi* of union with the guru's mind, the yogin vitalizes the psychic realities that the deities, their crowns, ornaments, and emblems represent. In this way the yogin identifies with the deity. This basic process is elaborated by the visualization of lights emanating and withdrawing from the yogin's heart, throat, and head centers (cakras) to their respective macrocosmic planes of reality represented by a Buddha. Further elaboration involves visualization of offerings to the deity, rites of confession, restoration of the samaya pledges (initiation vows), praise, and adoration. Finally, the vision is dissolved back into the emptiness out of which it arose.

Creative meditation should induce realization of the nature of relative truth (*samvrtisatya,* T. *kun-rdzob bden-pa,* "the truth that all is vanity"): that all phenomenal appearances are illusion and simply functions of our sensory apparatus; that no essential soul or *ens* persists; and that the universe is a system of interdependent relationships.

FULFILLMENT MEDITATION

Fulfillment meditation (*utpannakrama* or *nispannakrama*, T. *rdzogs-rim*) includes higher techniques of meditation that result in the understanding of ultimate truth (*paramarthasatya*, T. *don-dam bden-pa*). However, since relative and ultimate truth are two sides of the same coin, both the creative and fulfillment stages lead to the same goal.

Fundamentally, fulfillment meditation techniques entail the perception of emptiness in form, or the dissolution of form into emptiness. Specific fulfillment mode yogas are dream yoga; the yoga of the mystic heat (tumo); mahamudra meditation; the yoga of the apparitional body; the yoga of resurrection; clear light meditation; and the yoga of uniting skillful means and perfect insight to create the seed essence of pure pleasure.

The system of visualization vital in fulfillment meditation is that of the imaginary subtle body. This body consists of psychic nerves (*nadi*, T. *rtsa*); their focal points or energy centers (cakra T. *'khor-lo*); the energy that runs in the nerves (prana, T. *rlung*); and the essence of prana, "seed essence" (*bindu*, T. *thig-le*).

A central psychic energy channel or nerve (*avadhuti*, T. *dbu-ma*) runs from the sexual center to the fontanelle (crown of head); right, male *(rasana),* and left, female (*lalana*), channels run parallel, joining the central channel at the gut center. Converging from all parts of the body like physical veins, subsidiary nerves enter the central channel at the five focal points of psychic energy: the sexual, gut, heart, throat, and head centers.

While visualizing this system allows the yogin to manipulate the energies relating to the various centers for different mundane purposes, the main purpose is to inject all the streams of energy into the central channel and up to the head center, where ultimate liberation is achieved. The key to this system relates right and left channels to skillful means (male) and perfect insight (female), and the central channel to their union—mahamudra.

ACHIEVING MAHAMUDRA

In many of the legends it is stated that the guru's precepts instruct in both creative and fulfillment modes of meditation, but then in the verse of instruction, which is like a jewel in the plain narrative setting of the legend, it is often unclear how the instruction relates to the different modes. When this occurs, simply assume that "creative" and "fulfillment" modes indicate principles of meditation: the first that emptiness is form, and the second that all things are emptiness. For example, the skull cup symbolizes the first principle and its emptiness the second. Since creative meditation employs the extroversive energy of desire and relates to the father Tantra, while fulfillment employs the introversive energy of aversion and the death wish, and relates to the mother Tantra, the creative mode indicates radial energy and the fulfillment mode focal energy.

Mahamudra is attained by uniting the creative and fulfillment modes through practicing coincident meditation upon form and emptiness; practicing insight and concentration techniques simultaneously; uniting centripetal and centrifugal energies; uniting skillful means and perfect insight. Thus male and female principles, symbolized by creative and fulfillment modes, are united.

THE TRAPS OF DELUSION

Two quotes from sources antipathetic to the siddhas serve as illustrations here: "Do what thou wilt shall be the whole of the law." "Nothing is true; everything is permitted." The first is the dictum of Aleister Crowley, "The Great Beast," Britain's foremost practitioner of classical magic in the twentieth century. The second is from the Sufi master Hassan-i-Sabbah, who founded the assassin cult in Afghanistan in the eleventh century.

Both precepts could be accepted, with certain qualifications, by the siddhas. There is no limitation whatsoever to the siddhas' action *after* the experiential realization of pure awareness and emptiness, for the mystical experience of oneness ordains constant involuntary emanation of compassionate action. The siddha is only capable of acting for the benefit of all sentient beings. However, without this realization of the unity of self and other and the benign empathy with others that is its outcome, Crowley's dictum can very easily become a rationale for selfish, ambitious, power-hungry megalomaniacs.

Since ultimate reality is utterly inconceivable and unutterable there is no way to formulate "the real," or to separate it from the unreal. Since the temporal mind's functions create only delusion, and because "objective reality" is a function of the mind, the mind is only capable of delusively interpreting delusion. There is no solid ground anywhere:

All our conceptions of things are delusion,
For both the knower and his field of knowledge are
    unsubstantiated.
Since the fleeting moment is deceptive, there is no truth.

Thus, the siddha agrees with Hassan-i-Sabbah that "nothing is true," and he will agree with the corollary that "everything is permitted." However, the siddha insists upon the same qualification that governs the acceptance of Crowley's maxim. In order to prevent antisocial abuse of power there must first be a dissolution of "I" and "mine" into emptiness, a process of ego loss that implies the evaporation of all ambition and of the desire to impose one's will upon others or to make emotional demands.

KARMA

It could be argued that the Assassin's vow of total obedience had an effect comparable to ego loss, but sooner or later retribution must have followed, and with it discovery of the fallacy in their master's dictum.

Even if one does manage to understand that the phenomenal world is a lie, that moral and social values are merely creations of the mind and that all truth is relative, this awareness does not automatically lead to transcendence of karma and freedom from its laws. Only perpetual experiential identification with emptiness—ultimate reality—gives that freedom.

In acting upon the proposition that "all is permitted," those who have karmic debts to work through—the amoral materialist, the Machiavellian politician, the sensualist, even the obedient disciples of an ambitious teacher—are still subject to the inexorable though often unfathomable vicissitudes of karma. However, for the siddha who can relax constantly in the ultimate space of awareness, contemplating the river's flow with detachment, acting spontaneously without thought or effort, action makes no ripples. The siddhas' action is not our ordinary action, although it may appear so on the surface. Quite the contrary is true, for their action is styled "nonaction."

Much like the Taoist concept of nonaction (*wu-wei*), it is unmotivated and objectless. Egoistically motivated action is an attempt to divert the river's flow for personal or social advantage. Like a stone thrown in a still pond, these actions create ring upon ring of cause and effect that inevitably flood back upon the one who disturbed the calm depths of the flow. This is how karma works.

By contrast, the activity of the siddhas is in such harmony with the universal flow that they may appear to be the agents of a universal imperative. They may also appear to be magicians pulling the planets and stars out of their cosmic hats or conductors orchestrating nature's symphony. This is why the siddhas' inevitable, necessary, and absolutely specific nonaction is said to be "selfless activity for the sake of all beings."

THE HOLY MADMAN

But what of the siddhas' craziness, their lack of emotional inhibitions, their flouting of social conventions? For the siddhas themselves, all actions have the same value. It is only the prejudices and limitations of the observer's dualistic mind that see one set of actions as harmonious, selfless and "divine" and another as unconventional, outrageous, or insane.

Although nonaction is not limited by the parameters of social convention, it is limited by the siddhas' preparatory training. This is where the value of physical, moral, and mental training preparatory to initiation and the experience of ego loss becomes clear. After enlightenment there is no way to change the style and quality of how this reality manifests. The social intolerance toward the holy madman or enlightened clown can cramp the style of siddhas who forgot to do their homework.

It is up to the guru to make sure that the candidate for initiation is not going to be a liability to the lineage. The guru can be sure that the compassion injected into the initiate's bloodstream at the time of his enlightenment experience precludes demonic activity on the part of his initiate. However, the initiator must take great care when accepting candidates whose behavior after ego loss could be a danger to themselves. There is no fine line between divine craziness and total insanity—it is only a matter of degree.

THE PARADISE OF THE DAKINIS

All the siddhas who attained mahamudra-siddhi "finally attained ultimate liberation in the Paradise of the Dakinis." The final line in some legends is ambiguous when it states that the siddhas rose into paradise in their own bodies. This could mean that their bodies dissolved into light and thus their demise was a magical spiraling into the empyrean. Alternatively, it could also be a metaphorical rendering of their lives following enlightenment, that in the ultimate mystical experience they attained the pure land where existence was seen as a constant dance with the dakinis, the embodiment of the empty awareness of their continuous pleasure.

The siddhas who did not attain paradise were, for the most part, those who only attained mundane siddhi, which gave them immortality or extraordinary longevity so they could remain on earth working for humanity. These were the Nath siddhas who were to become recognized as the progenitors of the great hathayoga tradition of Saivite Tantra. The belief that they are still alive today is shared by millions of contemporary Hindus. They would very likely direct the inquirer to the Kumaon or Garhwal districts in the Himalayas to find Gorakhnath, Caurangi, and the other immortals who are believed to be still meditating in secluded caves.

THE LEGACY OF TANTRA

The legends convey the flavor of India in the eighth to the twelfth centuries, as well as the timeless ethos of Hindu spirituality. But their psychological core has a universal appeal and application that transcends culture, religion, and race. Aspects of Tantra can be found in the mysticism of every culture, and the systematic formulation of mysticism (insofar as mysticism can be rationalized) that is Tantra touches responsive chords in contemporary Western society.

The Western mystical mind most receptive to the tantric message of the siddhas is one with a strong repugnance against materialistic attitudes, the social and professional rat race, and the tedium of repetitive routine. Candidates for initiation might be people suffering from nervous anxiety, or facing a psychological breakdown, or considering entering analysis. Their minds should already be free from the emotional and conceptual constraints that hinder faith in the irrational or trust in a guru. They should be intelligent enough to be able to grasp simple metaphysical concepts, and sufficiently self-disciplined to sit in contemplation. If they have no knowledge of the sanctity of sex, they should at least be free of prudish or prurient attitudes. If they also happen to have contempt for scholasticism and pedantry and a healthy disrespect for intellectual analysis, as well as some disdain for secular authority, institutional discipline, social convention, and sacred cows, they are very well prepared for initiation into the siddhas' path.

A major obstacle on the path of Tantra for the Western mind deeply conditioned by a rational and scientific education is attachment to the law of the excluded middle. While this law—which insists upon a categorical positive or negative answer to any question—may be of enormous practical significance in the technological world, it is a radical impediment to gnostic awareness. Mahamudra-siddhi is only accessible when such thought patterns have become dominated by a vision that no longer experiences reality as this or that, or a synthesis of this and that, or an absence of this or that. Reality, in fact, *is* the excluded middle.

Although Westerners may possess the requisite receptivity, attitudes, and experience, they must still find a guru. A divine Bodhisattva or a dakini may appear to them propitiously. However, unless a great deal of preliminary work has been done on the mind, and unless a very strong working relationship is established with the divine agency, the instruction received from such a source can only be very simple and straightforward.

The principal bearers of the siddhas' tradition today are Tibetan lamas. To our good fortune, they are now seeking refuge in hospitable countries around the globe because of the Red Chinese invasion of Tibet and the need that they fill wherever they settle.

The Tibetan school that has retained the siddhas' ethos, as well as transmission of an uncorrupted though modified teaching tradition, is the Kagyupa school. To this school belongs the Tibetan classic, *The Songs of Milarepa,* which embodies the siddhas' teaching as interpreted by Milarepa and his guru Marpa, who received instruction from Naropa in the eleventh century.

There are lamas in the West today who have received the Milarepa tradition through the lineage of the late Gyalwa Karmapa. The Sakya school, in particular, has transmitted the mahamudra teaching of the siddha Virupa. The Nyingma school bases its doctrines upon the instruction of the *mahasiddha* Padmasambhava. And there is hardly an Indian-originated Tibetan lineage that does not include a name found among the eighty-four mahasiddhas.

The Tibetan tradition is characterized by an overwhelming unwillingness to question Indian doctrines and established values, and departures from the Tantra of the siddhas have been few and far between. Essential doctrine and practices remain fundamentally unaltered. The main difficulty is that while the lamas will teach the sadhanas, they will rarely spontaneously initiate untutored

Western aspirants and grant them precepts. Most lamas will insist upon a lengthy period of preparation in the disciplines of hinayana and mahayana Buddhism as well as preparatory tantric meditation practice.

However, the siddhas' tradition is still very much alive, and the next generation in the West will doubtless enjoy the fruit of the lamas' work. Since need, ability, and aspiration are present in a favorable environment, there is no reason countless American and European siddhas should not flourish in a latter-day blooming of the tantric tradition in the West.

KEITH DOWMAN,
MAY 1989

The Mahasiddhas

MINAPA
The Bengali Jonah

I am called Minapa, the stubborn fisherman.
When plunged into the vast sea of my destiny,
I survived in the belly of the holy Leviathan
By practicing a yoga meant for Umadevi alone.
After this, even solid rock
Could not bear the weight of my excellence.

Minapa the fisherman spent his life in a little craft out on the Bay of Bengal. Day after day, he would bait his hooks with morsels of meat, cast out his lines of homespun cotton, and wait for the tug that meant he had connected with a creature from the depths.

One bright, calm day, Minapa was plying his trade as usual, waiting patiently for a bite. Suddenly, there came a pull on his fishing line of such enormous strength that the poor little fisherman was yanked headlong into the sea. Minapa had hooked the most gigantic sea creature he had ever seen in his life. And once the Leviathan had seen the fisherman, Minapa became the bait on his own hook. The creature swallowed him whole. But so beneficent was his karma and so remarkable his luck, that the fisherman survived to set up house in the belly of the great fish.

Meanwhile, in the more celestial realms, Umadevi, Divine Consort of Siva Mahadeva, had taken it into her mind to learn her spouse's purest and most secret yogic practices. Night and day, she pleaded and begged and insisted, until Mahadeva knew he would have no peace until he instructed his consort in his dharma.

Yet until now his practices had been only for himself. He was uneasy about imparting teachings of such great power lest they fall upon the wrong ears. Therefore, he imposed one stricture. He would instruct Umadevi as she had requested, but he would only do so in the uttermost depths of the sea.

Umadevi was delighted. She immediately set about constructing an underwater hermitage of the most exquisite sacred shells, all hung about with pearls and precious corals. It was set within a garden of rare and delicate sea grasses and flowers, and she invited all manner of brightly colored fish to come and share her retreat. When he saw it, Mahadeva pronounced it suitable and immediately began his discourse.

Drawn by the amazing numbers of tempting fish, the Leviathan also took up residence in the neighborhood. And the deep and ringing tones of Mahadeva's precious words passed easily through the shell walls of the dwelling and through the flesh walls of the great fish. Unknown to Mahadeva, he acquired a rapt and faithful pupil.

Unfortunately, the same could not be said for Umadevi herself. Once she had gotten her way, the gentle movements of the undersea currents, and the hypnotic waving of the long sea grasses made her drowsy. Before long she nodded off. When Mahadeva asked her if she was listening, it was actually Minapa who replied, "Of course."

When Mahadeva reached the end of his instruction, the silence woke Umadevi. To cover her lapse, she said, "This is fascinating, my Lord, please continue."

"I just this moment informed you that I had finished," he said sharply.

"Perhaps I just dozed off for a moment or two," she admitted sheepishly.

"Then who answered 'Of course' when I asked if you were paying attention?"

"I did," came a small voice from out of the deeps.

With his magical gift for seeing through all things, Mahadeva soon spied Minapa in the belly of the great fish. "Aha!" he cried. "Now I see who my true disciple is. It is to the fish dweller that I will give initiation, and not to you, my dear."

Whereupon Minapa took the vow and, without ever leaving the belly of the great-spirited fish, began a twelve-year sadhana. At the close of this period, the Leviathan fell prey to the nets of an enterprising fisherman from Sri Tapari. Certain that the heaviness of the creature meant it had somehow swallowed enormous fortunes of silver and gold, the fisherman hacked it open with great effort.

The treasure that emerged was Minapa.

The poor fisherman was nearly frightened out of his wits. "Who are you?" he cried, staggering back.

To a gathering crowd Minapa related the tale of his capture and initiation.

And when he told them the name of the king in whose reign he had last seen the light of day, the astonished populace knew he had, indeed, lived in the belly of the great fish for twelve long years.

At this they gave him the name of Minapa, "The Fish Siddha," and prostrated themselves at his feet. They worshiped him with offerings, and a great feast was held right there on the sand where Minapa had emerged from the sea.

As though they had a mind of their own, Minapa's feet began to dance in an outburst of joy. Wherever his feet touched the rocky shore, they sank into the stone as though it were sun-warmed butter. To this very day you can still see the siddha's footprints embedded in solid rock.

As he danced, Minapa sang this song to his amazed audience:

> The source of my magic is twofold:
> It arises from the good fortune that accrued
> From the virtue of my past lives,
> And also from my steady devotion
> To the great teachings I have heard.
> Ah, my friends, what a precious jewel
> Is one's own mind.

Progressing along the path, Minapa worked selflessly for others for five hundred years. In time he came to be called Vajrapada, or Acintapa, and increased his magical powers manyfold. At last, his labors done, he arose bodily into the Paradise of the Dakinis.

LUIPA
The Fish-Gut Eater

Rub honey on a wild dog's nose
And it madly devours whatever it sees;
Give the lama's secret to a worldly fool
And his mind and the lineage burn out.

For a sensitive person who understands unborn reality,
One glimpse of the lama's vision of pure light
Destroys illusion like a mad elephant
Rampaging through hostile ranks, wielding a sword in its trunk.

When the old king of Sri Lanka died, the court astrologers determined that for the well-being of the kingdom only his second son could rule. But the young prince was loath to ascend the throne. He felt only disgust for the pomp and luxury of the palace. Contempt filled his eyes when he gazed at the walls of the royal chamber, plated with gold and silver and studded with precious stones.

All that he had ever wanted was to become a yogin, and he made up his mind to escape. But alas, his face was known to all, and the royal fugitive got no farther than the palace gardens. He was seized and bound in golden chains by his brothers and all the courtiers. The following night he bribed the guards with gold and silver and, disguised in rags, with only a single attendant, he made good his escape. Once they had journeyed some distance from the capitol, he rewarded his faithful servant generously and set out for Ramesvaram, where he began life as a yogin.

The yogin-king was more than delighted to exchange the golden throne of the palace for a deerskin mat and his royal silk-upholstered bed for a pile of

ashes. His beauty and charm made begging for his daily needs easy. His refinement and courtly manners inspired awe wherever he went.

The yogin wandered through India until he reached Vajrasana, the holy place where the Buddha Sakyamuni had achieved enlightenment. There, he became a devotee of the dakinis, who instructed him in the ways of feminine insight. Later, he journeyed to the royal city of Pataliputra on the river Ganges, where he studied the teachings of Tantra, lived on alms, and slept on a cremation ground.

One day, as he was begging in the bazaar, some inner sense told him to enter a tavern that also happened to be a brothel. It was his karmic destiny to meet one of the prostitutes there who was actually a dakini incarnate. He recognized her at once and paid her homage. The dakini gazed deeply into his mind for some time in utter silence. Then she said: "Your four psychic centers and their energies are quite pure. However, there is a knot of arrogance about the size of a pea in your heart." At this, she poured some putrid food into his clay bowl and sent him on his way.

As the yogin left the brothel, he threw the inedible slop into the gutter, whereupon the dakini, who had been watching, called out mockingly, "How can a gourmet attain nirvana?"

The yogin was mortified. Could it be that his critical, judgmental mind, educated in the refined atmosphere of the palace, was still subtly active? Was it possible that he still perceived some things as intrinsically more desirable than others? Such flaws would stand in the way of his progress toward Buddhahood.

He decided then and there to destroy his prejudices and cleanse his thought patterns at their roots. For the next twelve years he dwelt on the banks of the Mother Ganga, begging his supper from the fishermen cleaning their catch. All he would accept from them was entrails they normally tossed to the dogs. Although the fisherfolk called him Luipa, "The Fish-Gut Eater," to the royal yogin his food was the nectar of pure awareness through which he discovered that the nature of all substances is emptiness.

Luipa became renowned far and wide and his deeds mentioned in the legends of Darikapa.

VIRUPA
Master of Dakinis

I, who live in spontaneous reality
Depend upon the Magnificent Symbol.
I, who exist in things as they are,
Without self, not thinking, not achieving,
Am saved from the pit of nihilism by existential self-awareness,
Am saved from an eternal heaven by absolute detachment.
I live in consummate pure delight and perfect awareness.

Virupa, the dakini master, was born in Bengal in the eastern province of Tripura, during the reign of King Devapala. When still a young child, he entered the celebrated Buddhist monastic academy of Somapuri. There he devoted his life to study and meditation with a thousand other pious monks and received the initiation and empowerment of the dakini Vajra Varahi, the Sow-Faced One.

Industriously, he recited her mantra twice ten million times for twelve long years. And yet, nothing happened. Not once in all those twelve years did he receive so much as a dream to indicate that he was making progress.

At last, Virupa became so disgusted with himself and his apparently useless practice, that he threw his rosary into the latrine. Naturally, when the time came for evening worship, he did not have his prayer beads. Suddenly, Vajra Varahi herself appeared before him in a shining vision. She handed him an exquisitely carved rosary and said:

"Child of Happiness, why are you so troubled? Keep up your practice, for you are blessed by me. If you would see clearly that things are neither this nor that, you must let go your wandering, critical thoughts. Strip your mind of illusion!"

Deeply inspired, Virupa renewed his practice of the spiritual discipline of his dakini-guru for another twelve years, gaining the supreme realization of mahamudra.

As he had attained power over the duality of life and death, he saw no contradiction in eating meat or drinking alcohol, although it was against the rules of his order. One day he asked his servants for pigeon pie, whereupon they caught a few of the pigeons that roosted in the eaves of the monastery, wrung their necks, and prepared them for the table.

However, an elderly monk noticed that the pigeons had disappeared. Shouting, "Let him who has the audacity to eat pigeons come forth," he ran to the great bell to call everyone to assembly.

"Surely none of us would do such an abominable thing!'" whispered the venerable monks in astonishment. But the abbot ordered a cell-to-cell search. Before long they came to Virupa, sitting down with happy anticipation to a meal of pigeon and wine. Outraged, the monks stripped him of his office and ordered him to leave the monastery.

Virupa removed his habit and laid it with his begging bowl before the image of the Buddha that he had worshiped for more than a quarter of a century and prostrated himself in homage before the image. Then he left by the monastery gate.

"Where are you going?" demanded the gatekeeper.

"I am told I no longer belong here. Therefore, I shall follow whatever path is provided for me," he replied.

All the monks of Somapuri gathered at the gate as Virupa approached the broad lotus-filled lake that bordered the monastery.

At the water's edge Virupa tested one of the lotus leaves with his foot and saw that it did not sink beneath his weight. Then, miraculously, with the Buddha's name upon his lips, he trod lightly from leaf to leaf until he reached the opposite shore.

Their hearts in their mouths, the monks of Somapuri stood watching his amazing feat. Then, with great remorse, they prostrated themselves before Virupa and, in humble devotion, begged him to return.

"Please explain to us why you killed our pigeons," they implored.

"That was simply an illusion, like all temporal phenomena," replied the master and told his servants to bring him a few scraps of pigeon wing. Taking the bits of feather and bone, he held them aloft. At a snap of his fingers the pigeons were restored to life, and even more beautiful than before, they soared into the heavens.

Virupa then left the monastery once and for all to become a yogin.

Wherever he went, awestruck witnesses told tales of his miraculous doings.

One of his first adventures occurred at the banks of the river Ganges, where Virupa beseeched Ganga Devi, the goddess of the river, to give him something to eat and drink, for he had traveled far. But she refused. Whereupon Virupa commanded the waters to part and marched across to the other bank.

By the time he reached the nearby town of Kanasata he was ravenous. Entering a tavern, he demanded a flagon of wine and a plate of rice, which he devoured with gusto. Then he roared for more drink, then more and more, until he had drunk the tavern dry. When the suspicious tavernkeeper asked him to settle his bill, Virupa offered her the sun in the sky. To seal his pledge, he took his *phurba* from his robes and thrust this magical dagger exactly halfway between the light and the darkness, thus transfixing the daystar so it could not continue on its course.

For the next two and a half days the town of Kanasata was plagued with continual daylight and unremitting heat. The crops withered in the field, and even the river began to shrink from her banks. Virupa, however, continued to drink, consuming five hundred elephant loads of spirits.

By this time the king himself was at his wit's end. As yet unaware of Virupa's presence, he commanded his minister to discover the cause of the endless, blinding sunlight, but his investigations were fruitless. Finally, the sun goddess herself appeared to the king in a dream, revealing that a siddha's debt to a woman in a tavern imprisoned her above his realm. To rid himself of this disaster, the king was forced to pay the debt. Thereupon, Virupa vanished and the sun moved once again across the heavens.

Next, Virupa traveled to the country of Indra, which was ruled by exceedingly devout Brahmins. They had built a massive stone image of Mahadeva, the Great God Siva, which stood 680 feet high. The keepers of the shrine demanded that Virupa bow down before the image.

"How can an elder brother bow down to his junior?" scoffed the master. The king of Indra, who had come to worship at the image, heard these words and gave Virupa an ultimatum: "Bow down or die."

"It would be a sin for me to bow down to this deity," Virupa insisted. "Then let the sin be upon me!" said the king.

As soon as Virupa placed his palms together in homage, the gigantic stone image cracked in two and a great voice shook the heavens, saying: "Your word is my command!"

"Then swear your allegiance to the Buddha," commanded Virupa.

"I hear and obey," roared the voice, and at once the ruined colossus was miraculously restored.

The rich offerings that had been heaped at the feet of Siva were now offered to Virupa. He summoned all the devotees of Lord Buddha and distributed the offerings equally among them. So great was this bounty that the people were sustained through famine, flood, and pestilence for many, many years.

Virupa continued on his wanderings and came at last to the town of Devikotta in eastern India. Unknown to the yogin, the people of this place had all become flesh-eating ghouls.

On the road into town, in search of his morning meal, Virupa encountered a pleasant-looking matron who offered to fill his bowl if he would accompany her to her home. Thinking she must live nearby, he followed her as she turned off the main road. But when the woman hurried on and on, and the track became narrower and more overgrown, Virupa grew uneasy. He called out to the woman and asked if they were near their destination.

"You are very near the end of your journey," cried the woman. And she turned upon him and transfixed him with her blood-red eyes. Held fast by her spell, Virupa could not move so much as a finger to help himself as a menacing crowd of ghouls materialized silently from the shadowy jungle and carried him off to the abandoned temple.

Imprisoned within the moldering structure, Virupa found himself in the company of a very young Brahmin boy. The lad had also been in search of food that morning when he too had had the misfortune to meet the same spellbinding fiend upon the road. Now he and Virupa were about to become offerings themselves in some horrible rite. They could hear blood-curdling howls and wild drumming outside as the ghouls whirled in their dance of death.

The boy began to weep, but Virupa comforted him and told him to sleep; all would be well by sunup. As the child's tears melted into dream, Virupa blessed him with a powerful mantra of protection.

At moonrise, two brawny fiends came to fetch their tender young victim. But try as they might, they were unable to move the sleeping child. He was rooted to the earth. The yogin, however, was sleeping on a wooden plank, and the two thugs just managed to lift it and carry him out to the circle of dancers.

Wakened by the drums, Virupa was still unable to move as they plied him with liquor. He could only watch as the drunken ghouls worked themselves into a frenzy, brandishing their ritual knives in readiness for slaughter.

But just as their blood-maddened screeches reached a crescendo, Virupa burst into laughter. Surprised, but amused, the dancers laughed all the louder. But their glee turned to horror when his terrible twelve-tone bellow—the laughter of Heruka—began to drown out their hellish merriment. As his howls grew louder and louder, the ghouls were convulsed with pain and clasped their hands to their ears. When they implored him to stop, Virupa told them he would do so only if they vowed to devote themselves to the teachings of the Buddha. When his deafening laughter rang out again, the ghouls prostrated themselves before him and swore to do his bidding.

At this Virupa rose. In his right hand, as if by magic, there appeared an enormous razor-sharp discus. Towering behind him stood the horrific presence of the Demon of the North. "Should you entertain the slightest thought of not renewing your pledge to the Buddha every day," said the master with a fiendish grin, "expect to lose a cup of blood each day you fall from the path. And should you turn away entirely from the Buddha's law and worship some other god, this discus will fly from the heavens and sever your head from your neck, and the Demon of the North will suck your veins dry."

The repentant ghouls groveled on the ground before Virupa to do him homage. The master then gave a mighty heave, and the discus mounted into the night sky. The demon followed after, and both were transformed into glittering constellations.

Virupa then went on his way, journeying the length and breadth of India. When, many years later, he returned to Devikotta, it had become a peaceful town filled with devout Buddhists. To celebrate Virupa's return, Mahadev, the Great God Siva, and Umadevi, his consort, devised a spectacular illusion in the yogin's honor.

As Virupa stood on the road, surveying the town, it doubled and tripled in size until it had become a magnificent city of half a million households. People poured from their homes to welcome Virupa with offerings, while from the Thirty-three Sensual Paradises and all the palaces of the gods there flowed an endless array of the most exquisite food for a huge feast of celebration.

And yet, the great dakini master was not to attain ultimate liberation until he had lived seven hundred years. But then, as the great discus hurled itself across the vastness of space, his labors at last completed, Virupa ascended to the Paradise of the Dakinis.

DOMBIPA
The Tiger Rider

The philosopher's stone
Transforms base metal into gold.
In the heart of the Great Jewel
Passion is transformed into pure awareness.

In his youth, Dombipa, the king of Magadha, was initiated by the guru Virupa into the meditation rites of the Buddha-deity Hevajra. This practice gave him many magical powers, yet he kept them hidden.

Although he was the most enlightened of rulers and treated each of his subjects as a father would treat his only child, his people never suspected that he was an initiate of the mysteries. They knew only that their king was an honest man who treated his subjects with an even hand.

But Magadha had great need of its initiate-king because it had been burdened with bad karma for generations. The people suffered from the seemingly endless ravages of war, poverty, crime, famine, and pestilence. Desirous of liberating his people from this fate, the king thought long and hard about the best way to bring this to pass. At last, he ordered the casting of a huge bronze bell, knowing that the sound of a bell has the power to drive out demons and purify the minds of those who hear it.

With much ceremony, the king had the great bell hung from the strongest branch of a venerable tree growing in the very heart of the royal city. Before all the people, the king instructed his chief minister thusly: "Whenever you see danger or poverty or disease, you must strike this bell with all your might."

The minister obeyed faithfully. And each time the thrilling tones of the bell filled the air, the karmic cloud that hung over the kingdom was dissipated more and more. Until, in time, the entire kingdom of Magadha and each heart dwelling there had been purified by the clarifying vibrations. Peace and prosperity, health and joy filled the land.

Many years later a troupe of low-caste wandering minstrels chanced to arrive in the royal city. Hearing of their presence, the king summoned them to sing and dance for him. All through the entertainment the king could not draw his eyes away from the face of one of the performers, a young girl of extraordinary purity and charm. Fair-skinned, with classical features and an innocent demeanor, this virgin of twelve was as yet untainted by the world. She had all the qualities of a lotus child, a *padmini,* and the king decided then and there to make her his spiritual consort.

Discovering that she was the daughter of the chief minstrel, the king summoned him to his presence. However, when he asked the man for his daughter, the minstrel could only stare at the king in open-mouthed disbelief. Finding his tongue at last, the minstrel replied, "You are the great king of Magadha. You rule eight hundred thousand households. We are low-caste wretches. No union is allowed between our kind and yours. How could you even entertain such a thought?"

The king, however, commanded that the girl be weighed. And the minstrel stood dumbfounded as the chief minister counted out her weight in gold and handed it to him.

For a spate of years their mystic union remained hidden from all. But in the twelfth year prying eyes and gossiping tongues discovered their secret. Like wildfire, the rumor that the king was consorting with a woman far beneath his status swept across the realm. The royal scandal brought the business of the kingdom to a halt. Despite all the years of the king's just and benevolent rule, his subjects refused to tolerate such a flagrant transgression of the age-old laws of caste. They insisted upon his abdication.

Entrusting his kingdom to his son and faithful ministers, the king disappeared into the jungle with his consort. There, in an idyllic hermitage, surrounded by all the fruits and creatures of the earth, they dwelt in blissful solitude. Undisturbed, for another twelve years they devoted themselves to the practice of tantric yoga.

But in the kingdom of Magadha, all was not well. Without the clarity and wisdom of the king, hardship returned. The great bell cracked, and war, pestilence, and famine once again ravaged the land. In despair the young king ordered a council to be convened. There it was decided that the old king should be asked to return, and a delegation was immediately dispatched into the jungle to find him.

For weeks the search party looked high and low, traveling into remote parts of the jungle unexplored in human memory. But there was no trace of the old king or his consort.

Finally, one day, lost and discouraged, ready to return home in failure, the youngest among them noticed something unusual. A vast silence had settled over the forest. No birds sang, no leaves rustled. All the world was perfectly still.

In the distance, they could just make out a faint glow. Moving silently in that direction, they came at last upon the king sitting under a tree by the shores of a lake, deep in meditation. There, in the middle of the lake, treading delicately upon a pathway of lotus leaves floating on the surface, was his consort. Gracefully, she bent and dipped her hand into the waters of the lake, and bubbling up from the amazing depth of fifteen fathoms there arose a fountain of shimmering nectar. Catching the divine liquid in her cupped hands, she traveled back across the lily pads to offer the drink to her lord.

Awe-stricken, the search party could not bring themselves to intrude upon the royal solitude. They rushed back to the city to report all that they had witnessed, and another delegation was dispatched to the king. They carried with them messages, pleas, and prayers from the length and breadth of the realm beseeching him to return.

The king received the envoys in his hermitage. Deeply moved by their tale of woe, the king agreed to return and help his suffering people. He told them to expect him a fortnight hence.

On the day of his return, thousands of people lined the route to the palace. To their astonishment, the king, brandishing a deadly snake as a whip, emerged from the shadowy jungle riding with his consort on the back of a pregnant tigress. Overcome with fear, the people fell to their knees and begged him to take up the reins of government once again.

"How can I possibly do as you ask," reasoned the king. "You drove me away because I had lost my caste status by consorting with a woman of low birth. Casteless, I cannot rule." When they began to bewail their cruel fate, the king took pity on them and said, "Since death ends all distinction, you must burn us together on a funeral pyre. In our rebirth we will be absolved."

A great pyre was constructed of the most fragrant and precious wood in the kingdom, cow-head sandalwood. Serenely, without a moment's hesitation, the king and his consort mounted to the top, and the wood was set afire.

For seven days it perfumed the air. For seven nights it lit the sky as brightly as any sun. On the eighth day the fire suddenly and mysteriously disappeared. As the people drew near, they were amazed to see, hovering in the air above the ashes, a lotus-shaped cloud of shimmering dewdrops. In the heart of this magical flower sat the king in the guise of the Buddha-deity Hevajra in ecstatic union with his consort.

At this the last vestiges of doubt fell from the minds of the people of Magadha. They gave their king the name Dombipa, "Lord of the Dombi," after his outcaste consort.

Emerging from the lotus cloud, the king addressed his ministers and all the people of his realm, the four castes gathered together. "If you can find it in your hearts to do as I have done," said the king, "I will stay to govern you."

Shocked, the populace protested, "We are not yogins. How can you ask us to give up our homes, our families, our way of life? How can you ask us to become casteless?"

The king sighed deeply and said, "How useless is political power, and how great the retribution for using it. Those who wield authority do very little good and more often do great harm."

As he spoke, the outlines of his form became increasingly transparent and insubstantial. His last words were: "My only kingdom is the kingdom of truth." Whereupon he dissolved into perfect awareness and pure delight, to dwell forever in the Paradise of the Dakinis.

SARAHA
The Great Brahmin

Never forget sahaja, the inborn absolute,
But seek for it only on the lips of the guru.
Realize that the ultimate nature of the guru's word
Is to make the body ageless and the mind eternal.

The Brahmin Saraha was the son of a dakini, and he was born in the east of India in Roli, a region of the city-state of Rajni. Saraha was himself a daka, a spiritual being, and had many magical powers. Observing the laws of the Brahmins by day, he received instruction in the tantric mysteries from many Buddhist masters by night.

However, Saraha enjoyed spiritous liquors, which were forbidden by Brahmin law. Eventually, this was discovered by his fellow Brahmins, and they were outraged by his behavior.

A delegation was sent to King Ratnapala to demand that Saraha be deprived of his caste status.

"How can you, a great king responsible for the religious purity of your country, allow Saraha, lord of fifteen thousand households, to dishonor his caste by drinking? You must excommunicate him," the puritans demanded.

The king, however, was a reasonable man. He decided to investigate the matter for himself and paid a private visit to Saraha. When he upbraided the miscreant for drinking, Saraha said, "I do not drink. If you doubt me, gather together the Brahmins and all the people and I'll prove it."

Before a great crowd, Saraha announced a series of trials to prove his innocence. Declaring, "If I am guilty, may my hand burn to the bone," he

plunged his hand into a vat of boiling oil. To the amazement of all, when he withdrew his hand several minutes later, it was entirely unharmed.

"This convinces me of his innocence," said the king, turning to the Brahmins. "Are you satisfied?"

"The charlatan drinks!" they shouted.

Whereupon Saraha called for a bowl of molten copper. "If I am guilty," he cried, "let my mouth and throat be horribly burned." And he drank the smoking liquid in one gulp. When he opened his mouth wide, the populace could clearly see healthy pink skin.

"Enough of these magic tricks!" shouted the Brahmins. "We know he drinks!"

Saraha then led the crowd to a huge tank of water. "Let him who is assured of his purity jump into this tank with me," Saraha challenged. "The one who sinks is the liar."

A Brahmin zealot shouldered his way through the crowd and offered himself for the test. When they both leaped into the tank, the Brahmin promptly sank to the bottom.

"Who dares to accuse me of drinking now?" shouted the dripping Saraha.

"If the slightest doubt still exists, weigh the two of us. Whoever is the lighter is guilty." The crowd gasped, for the Brahmin was twice the size of Saraha. But when the two were weighed, the scale showed that Saraha was much the heavier.

At this point, the king stepped in. Pointing to Saraha, he declared, "If this venerable being drinks, then may he continue to do so for all time." And the king prostrated himself before Saraha, followed by all the Brahmins, and the assembled crowd.

Saraha began to sing three song cycles: one to the king, one to the queen, and one to the people. After receiving Saraha's instruction, the Brahmins gave up their traditional practices and entered the path of the Buddha. In time the king, the queen, and the entire court attained Buddhahood. The songs that Saraha had sung became known far and wide as the "Three Cycles of Dohas" and achieved great fame.

As for Saraha himself, he took a fifteen-year-old girl as his consort and moved to a distant land. With the girl to beg for their daily needs, Saraha continued to practice his sadhana in isolation.

One day he told her to cook him a radish curry for supper. However, as she set about preparing it carefully with buffalo-milk curd, he began to meditate. He meditated all that night, and all the next day, and the day after that. He continued to meditate for twelve long years.

But the moment he again awakened to the outside world, he bellowed at the top of his lungs: "Where is my radish curry?"

"You sit in samadhi for twelve years and the first thing you ask for is radish curry?" asked his dakini consort in amazement.

Chastised, Saraha decided he must move to a mountain hermitage to continue his meditation properly.

"If you can awaken from samadhi with an undiminished desire for radish curry, what do you think the isolation of the mountains will do for you?" inquired his consort. "The purest solitude," she counseled, "is one that allows you to escape from the preconceptions and prejudices, from the labels and concepts of a narrow, inflexible mind."

Saraha listened carefully to the wisdom of his dakini-guru and began to devote himself exclusively to ridding his mind of conceptual thought and belief in the substantiality of objective reality. In time he began to experience all things in their primal purity, eventually attaining in boundless service to others. Upon his death, Saraha and his consort ascended to the bliss of the Paradise of the Dakinis.

LILAPA
The Royal Hedonist

Steadfast in the Four Stages of Boundlessness
Reigns the yogin-king—the royal snow lion.
The five plaits of his turquoise mane
Are the five-fold insignia of the Buddha's Awareness.
His lion's claws tear an ox's flesh from its bones
As the yogin's ten perfections cut through negative powers.
This is the realization that won Lilapa eternal freedom.

There was once in the south of India a hedonistic king who valued his pleasures and his treasures above all things. However, this king also enjoyed intelligent conversation, and from time to time visitors were invited into the royal chamber, where he reclined on his lion throne, dressed in the most sumptuous of garments.

One day a wise yogin came to the court and was granted an audience. When the king saw his tattered clothing and weathered face, he was filled with pity.

"What a terrible life you must lead, wandering from country to country in such a miserable state," he said.

"I have nothing to complain about," the yogin replied. "You are the one to be pitied."

"What makes you think such a thing?" asked the king, taken aback.

"I have eyes," said the yogin. "I can see that you live in constant dread of your own subjects. Above all, you fear the loss of your throne. But I, I am free from all suffering. The pain of old age, even death itself, is unknown to me. Were I to leap into a roaring fire, I would not be burned. Were I to swallow the deadliest of poisons, I would not die."

"How can this be?" asked the king, amazed.

"I have learned the great teachings of the alchemists," replied the venerable yogin. "I possess the secret of immortality."

The words of the yogin affected the king so profoundly that his faith was kindled on the spot. "I am unable to wander from place to place as you do," he said, "but if you could teach me how to meditate while remaining here on my throne in my palace I would be very grateful. I beg you to remain long enough to instruct me," and he prostrated himself in humble supplication.

The yogin granted the king's request by initiating him into the meditative practices of the deity Hevajra. The king learned to concentrate his attention unwaveringly upon the jeweled ring on his right hand. In time he was able to visualize within the heart of the jewel the great Hevajra himself seated amid his retinue of divinities. When the king succeeded in transfixing this vision he united both the creative and fulfillment modes of meditation, and the state of realization, the one-pointed trance of samadhi, spontaneously unfolded.

Thereafter the king meditated ceaselessly. The dawning of his understanding had endowed him with the power and realization of mahamudra as well as other abilities, such as extrasensory perception. Yet he accomplished all this while seated upon his lion throne, reclining on cushions of silk, surrounded by his queens and ministers, and entertained by the court musicians.

His fondness for sensual pleasures soon earned him the name Lilapa, which means "Master of Play." Nevertheless, he became known throughout the world for wonderful acts of selflessness and in the end gained the ultimate liberation of entering the Paradise of the Dakinis.

Lilapa's story shows us that when the karmic leanings and aspirations of the disciple blend harmoniously with the teachings of the guru, there is no need to renounce the pleasures of this life in order to attain liberation.

SAVARIPA
The Hunter

Hidden in the forest of unknowing
Waits the deer known as alienation.
Hunter, draw taut the bowstring of insight
On the bow of skilful means,
and let fly the arrow of ultimate truth:
Thus shall the deer fall and thought die.
When you feast upon the venison of nonduality,
Richly flavored with pure pleasure,
You shall know the goal of mahamudra.

On the slopes of Vikrama Peak, in the rugged Mantra mountain chain, lived Savaripa, a savage hunter. He was a man trapped in a vicious karmic cycle of killing to live and living to kill. Such is the fate of all hunters.

One day, however, he came to the notice of Lokesvara, the Bodhisattva of Compassion. Taking pity on him, the Bodhisattva decided to release Savaripa from his karmic curse. Assuming the form of a hunter, Lokesvara stood waiting for him on the road.

"And who might you be?" asked Savaripa, looking the newcomer up and down.

"I am a hunter, as you are," the stranger replied.

"Where from?" asked Savaripa suspiciously.

"Very far away," came the evasive reply.

Savaripa decided to put the stranger to the test. "If you had only one arrow," he challenged, "how many deer could you hit?"

"Oh, three hundred or so," replied the Bodhisattva calmly.

Savaripa snorted. "I'd like to see you try."

"Tomorrow at dawn then," said the Bodhisattva as he melted into the forest and vanished.

The next morning found Savaripa and the Bodhisattva far out on a vast plain in search of deer. Before long they came upon a herd of five hundred that had been secretly conjured up by Lokesvara.

"There are your deer," whispered Savaripa. "Let's see how many you can shoot."

"How about all five hundred?" asked his companion.

"Oh, I think a hundred would do as a start," said Savaripa mockingly. The Bodhisattva let fly a single arrow, and a hundred deer fell dead. Then he asked the astonished hunter to help him carry one home. Despite his strength, Savaripa's arms began to tremble as he attempted to lift the deer. Try as he might, he was unable to move so much as a leg of the dainty creature. With the last remnants of his pride gone, the deeply embarrassed Savaripa asked the Bodhisattva to teach him to use the bow as well as he did. Lokesvara agreed, but only on condition that Savaripa and his wife abstain from eating meat for an entire month. Savaripa agreed.

When barely a week had passed, the Bodhisattva returned and added another stipulation to their agreement: If Savaripa wanted archery instruction, he would have to meditate upon loving-kindness and compassion for all living creatures. Again, the hunter agreed.

When the month had passed, the Bodhisattva returned, and Savaripa welcomed him with delight. Lokesvara then drew a mandala in the dirt floor of the hunter's cabin and scattered it with flowers. "Look deeply into what I have drawn," he said to the hunter and his wife. "Tell me what you see."

As they gazed into the magic circle, the couple turned ashen and shut their eyes tight in dismay. Neither man nor wife could speak.

"Tell me what you see," demanded the Bodhisattva.

"Ourselves, burning in the eight great hells!" Savaripa finally blurted out.

"Are you not filled with fear?" asked the Bodhisattva.

"Yes. Oh, yes," gasped the couple.

"What would you do to avoid it?"

"Anything!"

Whereupon their visitor began to explain the basic tenets of the Buddha's doctrine. Savaripa began to understand why he had been asked to stop eating meat and to contemplate compassion for all forms of life. He now realized that killing only strengthened the desire to kill again. The result was that society looked upon such people as dishonorable and vile. And the karmic retribution for such a life was rebirth in a human hell.

"If you foreshorten the lives of others," the Bodhisattva explained, "you can expect your own life to be cut short before its time. Why not give up hunting altogether and devote your life to the search for enlightenment? As the desire to kill diminishes, you will begin to accumulate immense merit and virtue." At this the hunter and his wife vowed to follow the path of the Buddha.

Over time the Bodhisattva instructed the couple on the karmic effects of virtue and vice and taught them the ten virtuous actions. He also demonstrated how retribution was inevitable for all unpropitious acts. Then he showed them how to live a joyous, healthy life.

Filled with remorse and disgust for his past life, Savaripa retired to Danti Mountain to meditate upon the correct way to escape the suffering inherent in the revolutions of the Wheel of Life. After twelve years in a sublime thought-free state of undirected, unstructured compassion, Savaripa attained the supreme realization of mahamudra.

The former hunter then sought out his Bodhisattva-guru for further instruction. After praising his achievement, Lokesvara looked into his pupil's future, saying, "Worldly one, your release is not the single-minded nirvana of those who choke passion at the root like a shepherd stomping out a grass fire. Remain instead upon the Wheel of Rebirth out of compassion for all those still bound to it. By so doing, you will save an infinite number of souls."

Savaripa willingly agreed and returned to his own country. In time he came to be called Majigochen, "The Peacock-Feather Wearer" and also Ritro Gompo, "Keeper of the Mountain Hermitage." Today he still teaches those fortunate enough to understand his message through song and dance, sound and symbol. And so it shall be until the day when Maitreya, the Buddha of Love—the Buddha Yet to Come—begins to teach the gospel of the New Age.

GORAKSA
The Immortal Cowherd

Whatever your birth—high, middle, or low—
Use the circumstances of your life
To the fullest. Realize the flow
Of karma is helping you reach your goal.
I seized my chance for enlightenment
In faithful service to Caurangi, the Limbless One.
Then Acinta served me the nectar of immortality
And I beheld nondual reality.
Now I have become the Cowherd King of Three Realms.

During the reign of King Devapala, a poor incense seller in the eastern part of India was forced to hire out his youngest son, Goraksa, as a cowherd. It was a humble, simple life, but the boy enjoyed the countryside and the gentle company of the animals.

One lazy afternoon he was lying in the tall grass talking with some of the other cowherds when, suddenly, a towering form appeared before them. It was the mahasiddha Minapa, known also as Acintapa. The guru pointed into the distance and in a ringing voice asked, "Do you see the vultures circling over there? They are awaiting the death of a young prince who lies gravely wounded in the shade of a lone tree. He has been set upon, and his arms and legs have been cut off. Who will save him and care for him?"

Instinctively seizing the moment, Goraksa cried, "I will," and leapt to his feet. "But if I do your work for you," he said to Minapa, "you must do mine for me."

And so the bargain was struck. Minapa remained to watch the herd, and the boy ran off toward the cloud of vultures. Before long, he discovered the limbless victim, whose lifeblood was seeping into the roots of the tree beneath him. Goraksa cleaned and bound the terrible wounds with bandages torn from his own clothes. After he had done what he could to make the prince comfortable, he returned to Minapa and reported all that he had seen and done.

"Will you find a way to feed him?" asked the guru.

"Yes," the boy replied. "The owner of my herd gives me food and drink morning and evening. I will give the prince half of what I receive."

The guru praised Goraksa and gave him instructions for the care of the prince. "In order to live, he must perform the four basic functions of life: eating, drinking, sleeping, and defecating."

The humble cowherd went back to the prince and used the branches and leaves of the tree to build a protective shelter around him. Each day thereafter, as they both grew to manhood, Goraksa shared his food and drink with him. And he bathed the prince, and cleaned away the excrement, and did all that was needed for the prince's comfort.

One beautiful evening, twelve years later, when the setting sun was painting the darkening sky with glorious crimsons and golds, Goraksa was bringing the prince his evening meal as usual. But when the simple cowherd arrived at the tree shelter, he saw the most incredible sight.

Openmouthed, Goraksa watched as the prince stood up from the spot where his limbless body had remained motionless for all those long years. Now he was standing on two strong, healthy legs and stretching out two muscular arms.

"You'd better close your mouth," said the prince sharply. "You'll swallow a fly." Whereupon he levitated into the air and hovered just over Goraksa's head. "Minapa has taught me a yoga that has caused my limbs to regenerate. In repayment for your service I am willing to teach you how to meditate."

"Thank you, my lord, but no," replied Goraksa. "I already have a guru serving you all these years, I have simply been obeying his instructions."

And the faithful cowherd returned to his grazing animals. Before long, Minapa appeared before him and inquired after his charge. Goraksa told him of the prince's miraculous restoration. The guru was delighted and praised the young man's diligence and faithfulness. Then and there he gave Goraksa initiation and empowerment and carefully instructed him in the precepts he should follow.

Goraksa then traveled to a distant land where he could practice meditation according to Minapa's instruction. When he attained the more mundane level of awareness, Minapa appeared before him again. "You cannot attain complete awakening and the purity of Buddhahood," said the guru, "until you have liberated one hundred million beings."

Such was Goraksa's enthusiasm for service that he rushed off into the world and began initiating anyone who would stop and listen to him. However, in his eagerness, he neglected to make a careful assessment of his students' ripeness for instruction.

This upset the Great God Mahedeva, who appeared before Goraska as he sat amid a crowd of initiates. Reproving him, Mahadeva warned the cowherd, "Instruct only those who come to you and request your teachings. Never initiate those who lack faith or true understanding."

Thereafter, Goraksa taught only those whose karma had prepared them for initiation, yet he still liberated countless numbers of people. To this very day Goraksa, whose name means "Protector of the Herd," continues to teach. Those who are pure in mind and ready for instruction hear the steady beat of his drum. But to others, he will forever remain silent and unseen.

TANTIPA
The Senile Weaver

Stringing my warp and woof,
Guided by the guru's precepts,
I weave patterns of experience
From the invisible thread of fivefold awareness.

With my shuttle of the guru's instruction
and my loom of perfect insight into emptiness,
I weave the cloth of dharmakaya
From endless space and the play of pure knowledge.

There was once a fine weaver who made his home in Sendhonagar. He worked hard and built up a prosperous trade. In due time he imparted his skills to his many sons, and their talents and industriousness brought great wealth to the family. As the years passed, the sons all married, taking wives from their own caste, and the tribe of weavers increased in the land.

When the weaver was eighty-nine years old, his beloved wife died. His sad loss aged him swiftly. He soon grew senile and infirm and was unable to care for himself. His daughters-in-law took it upon themselves to feed and tend to the old man, but they constantly fussed and complained about him to their husbands.

One said, "His foolishness is a constant source of embarrassment when customers come to call."

Another said, "The whole town makes fun of him—and us. He's ruining our reputation."

Yet another said, "He's creating negative karma for the whole family. Do you want your children and grandchildren to be poor as field mice?"

Finally, all the sons said to their wives, "Do as you will with him. Only leave us in peace."

The wives conferred. They were all much too good-hearted to turn the old man out, but they wanted him out of sight. At last one of them had the idea to build him a cool and comfortable grass hut out in the garden. There no one would see him, but he would be in beautiful surroundings. They all agreed on this plan.

Thus the old man was banished from house, home, and family. And although his daughters-in-law continued to feed him as before, he grew bitter and angry. Lonely in his grass hut, he took to talking to the passing breezes.

One day, some months after his banishment, it happened that the guru Jalandhara was passing through Sendhonagar. Among those he approached for food was the weaver's eldest son. The son invited him to his home for a meal, where his wife was only too pleased to serve the holy man. After the guru had dined, the wife invited him to stay the night. He refused, saying that it was not his custom to sleep on comfortable beds indoors. Graciously, his hostess let him out into the scented cool of the night garden. She had her servants fetch him a lamp and anything else he might require and bade him good night.

Just as Jalandhara was falling asleep, he heard a tremulous old voice speaking fretfully to itself. "Hello?" he called out.

There was a moment of silence. Then the disembodied voice demanded imperiously, "Who's that!"

"A visiting mendicant," replied the yogin. "Who are you?"

"The head of this household, that's who!" came the querulous reply. Lighting his lamp, Jalandhara suddenly spied a small grass hut nearly hidden by a wild growth of sweet-smelling jasmine. He entered the hut and, at the old man's invitation, sat down and listened to the weaver's tale of woe.

"I am the father of this family of weavers. In my prime I was the master of this house and business, but no one has any use for me now," the old man complained. "I have been humiliated by my own sons and their wives. They keep me locked up in this hut as though I were some kind of monstrosity. How hollow are life's promises!"

The guru sat thinking for a moment. And then he said, "Everything we make or do is but a passing show. Everything that enters into existence enters into suffering. Everything is hollow illusion. Only in nirvana can peace and happiness be found. Would you like me to give you the instruction that prepares one for death?" he asked.

"I would," replied the weaver, his voice firm and sure.

Whereupon the guru initiated him into the mandala of Hevajra and taught him how to meditate.

The following morning the guru departed, and life went on as usual. No one cared or realized that the old man had begun to practice the precepts of his meditation, although they did notice that he no longer complained about his fate. In fact, he no longer spoke at all.

Twelve years passed in perfect silence in the hut. But during this time the old weaver attained certain powers. This remained secret until one day when the family was celebrating the completion of an exquisitely luxurious carpet commissioned by their wealthiest patron.

Suddenly, in the midst of the feasting, the wife of the eldest son remembered that she had forgotten to bring food to her father-in-law at the usual time. Thinking that the silly, mute old man must be faint from hunger by now, she rushed off with a platter of food.

But no sooner had she entered the hut than she froze in amazement. The platter fell from her hands as she beheld the weaver suffused in lamplike radiance. He was sitting in a circle of fifteen beautiful girls who were adorned in ornaments and gossamer fabrics unknown in the human realm. Each girl was holding a dish of the most sumptuous food, feeding the weaver with her fingers.

When the eldest son's wife came to herself, she ran back to the family as fast as she could go, crying, "Come to the garden . . . the garden . . ."

Thinking his father must be dying, the eldest son began to weep, and the whole family hurried to the hut. There, they were nearly blinded by the radiance that now filled the entire garden. "The old man is possessed!" they shouted.

By morning the entire city of Sendhonagar had heard the amazing tale of the old weaver in the garden. People came from every quarter to stare. Some prostrated themselves before the hut.

At last the weaver emerged from his place of exile. But he was a senile, decrepit old man no longer. He had been transformed into a sixteen-year-old boy, bursting with strength and health. The transfiguring light that emanated from him was so intense that the onlookers were forced to cover their eyes. His body was like a highly polished mirror, and all manifest appearances were reflected from him as pure light.

The weaver became known as the guru Tantipa. After numerous years spent in selfless acts for the populace, he was assumed into the Paradise of the Dakinis along with a vast host from the city of Sendhonagar.

KHADGAPA
The Master Thief

Persevere as he will,
The warrior without weapons
Will always be defeated.
But, armed with the sword of Undying Awareness,
I vanquish my enemies, the demons
Of the three Realms, without regrets.

When a son was born into a low-caste family of farmers in the kingdom of Magadha, everyone rejoiced. But as the boy grew older, the family's joy turned to sorrow. Day by day it grew more apparent that Khadgapa had no use for the industrious ways of his forefathers. All his talents were devoted to thievery.

And, it must be said, those talents were prodigious. He could steal an egg a chicken had yet to lay. While he certainly enjoyed the benefits of his profession, it was the thrill and danger of it all that gave him the most pleasure.

As he honed his craft, his exploits became more and more daring. One day he decided to pilfer a legendary ruby from the richest man in Magadha. All went well until, just as he was about to make a getaway with his prize, he trod on the tail of a sleeping cat. The ensuing noise brought the entire household in pursuit of Khadgapa, who dropped the ruby as he fled for his life.

As luck would have it, a funeral cortege happened to be passing through the neighborhood, and our master thief slipped in among the mourners, beating his breast and wailing with the rest. Try as they might, his pursuers could not distinguish him from the others and it would have been indelicate to disturb the mourners.

Khadgapa followed the bereaved family all the way to the cremation ground,

giving heartfelt thanks to the departed for saving his life. He decided to lie low in the cremation ground for several days for safety's sake, and while he was there he chanced to meet the yogin Carpati practicing his sadhana.

"Who are you hiding from?" the thief asked the yogin.

"I'm trying to dodge the repetitive cycle of birth and death on the Wheel of Existence," replied Carpati. "So I'm meditating."

"I don't get it," said the thief. "Where's the payoff?"

"There's a big payoff," said the yogin. "I will attain a higher state of existence, and on top of that, I will gain the happiness that is the fruit of absolute certainty."

"Well and good for you," said the thief.

"You can have it too," said Carpati, "if you practice the Buddha's teaching."

"I respect the Buddha's teaching," said Khadgapa. "But I certainly haven't got time to sit around on my rump all day meditating in a cremation ground. I don't suppose you'd happen to know a siddhi of invincibility that would protect me when I'm pulling a caper—even if I steal from the king?"

"As a matter of fact, I do," said the guru. Whereupon he gave the master thief initiation and empowerment. And then he instructed him in this manner:

"In a city in Magadha there is an old temple called Gauri-sankar. It looks like a stupa from the outside, but it's actually a shrine containing a statue of Avalokitesvara. When you enter you will sense that it is highly charged with the Bodhisattva's grace.

"Your sadhana," the guru continued, "is to walk in circles around the statue day and night for twenty-one days. You must stop for nothing. Even when you eat you must continue to walk around the statue. After you have done this faithfully for twenty-one days, be on the lookout for a large snake that will glide out between the feet of the statue. The moment you see it, you must seize it by the head. If you show any fear or hesitation, all is lost. Bu do as I say, you will gain the siddhi you desire."

The thief soon learned which city contained this temple, and he journeyed there as fast as he dared. Since he was still a hunted man, he could only move safely in the dead of night. Finally, he arrived at the temple door.

When he entered, he was suffused with the presence of the Bodhisattva, just as his guru had said. Encouraged by this, Khadgapa began walking around the statue. Day and night, night and day, for twenty-one days, he followed his guru's instructions to the letter. Around and around and around the statue of

Avalokitesvara he walked until his pain and fatigue evaporated like morning mist.

On the evening of the twenty-first day of his sadhana, a large black snake uncoiled itself from the Bodhisattva's feet and began to glide slowly across the floor. In a trice the fearless thief seized it by the head.

No sooner was the serpent in his hand than there came a ferocious thunderclap and a blinding flash of light. And there, held firmly in Khadgapa's fist, was the most beautiful sword he had ever beheld. The longer he held it, the more radiantly it glowed. In this clear light all shadows were dispelled. Suddenly, all the defiling delusions of Khadgapa's mind were made as palpable, as visible to him as the snake he had grasped.

And as he beheld these shadows of the mind, the cutting edge of the light severed them from his being. In one and the same moment he was free of defilement and gained the siddhi of the sword, one of the eight great magical powers. Forever after he was called Khadgapa, which means "The Swordsman."

For the next twenty-one days, the former thief taught the Buddha's message to all the people of Magadha. He then expressed his realization and was assumed into the Paradise of the Dakinis.

CAURANGIPA
The Limbless One

From time without beginning, the tree of unknowing
Has been watered by the monsoon of mental habit.
What a tangle of delusion it has become.
Listen. Ponder. Practice.
Chop it down with the ax of the guru's instruction.

Caurangi was the son of Devapala, an East Indian king. While his father was a kindly man, the youth was also much attached to his saintly mother. When he was only twelve she was stricken with a fatal disease, and he was summoned to her deathbed. With her last breath she offered him the essence of her teachings. "All joys and sorrows are rooted in two kinds of actions—vicious and virtuous," she counseled him. "Even if your life is at stake, never do evil." So saying, she died.

Within the year, the king took a young and beautiful woman as his wife, but he also continued his meditational practices. One day, not long after their marriage, the king retired for a time to his jungle retreat. The lonely young queen wandered about the palace familiarizing herself with her new domain and in the cool of the evening climbed up to the roof of the palace to enjoy the view.

By chance a sound in the courtyard below caught her attention. Gazing down, her eyes fell upon the young prince. For the first time she noticed his great beauty, and her heart began to pound in her breast. In the space of a moment she had become completely infatuated with him.

Burning with desire, the queen sent one of her serving maids down to the prince with an amorous invitation. But Caurangi was taken aback. With scant politeness, he refused the queen's invitation.

When her servant returned with the prince's refusal, the queen was mortally humiliated. All her passion was immediately transformed into fury. "Let him despise me," she thought. "He'll rue this day, mark my words." She spent a tormented night, filled with dreams of passion and revenge. In the morning her anger was undiminished. She summoned her retainers and proposed a plan to do away with the prince. But they had known him since birth and loved him deeply.

"The prince is innocent," they objected. "He is only a child. He does not deserve to die."

The queen was livid. Her desires frustrated at every turn, she resorted to deception. Learning that the king was expected momentarily, she dismissed her servants, turned her bedroom upside down in wild array, tore off her clothes and inflicted bloody scratches all over her body. When the king entered her chambers, he found her weeping hysterically.

"Who has done such a thing to you?" demanded the king.

"Your son," she moaned. "When I tried to resist, he . . ."

"He is no longer my son," cried the anguished king. "He must die." Summoning two faithful servants, the distraught father ordered them to take his son deep into the jungle. There they were to cut off all his arms and legs and leave him to bleed to death or to be devoured by great beasts. The queen demanded that they return bearing the severed limbs as proof that they had carried out the king's will.

Once out of the king's presence, the two servants burst into tears. They loved the innocent prince even more than their own children and drew lots to see which of their sons they would sacrifice instead. But when they came to the prince with their plan, he told them what his dying mother had taught him.

"I cannot let another die in my place," said the prince. "It would be a sin. You must obey my father's command."

Convulsed with sobs, the two servants decided to at least avoid the perils of the jungle. And they conveyed the doomed prince to a distant place just on the edge of a grassland where there were sure to be villagers nearby. At least he would have some faint promise of hope.

Feeling all the pain of their young charge as they severed his arms and legs from his body, the unwilling executioners propped him against the lone tree they had found, and gathered up the useless limbs to bring back to the vengeful queen.

No sooner had they disappeared over the horizon than the yogin Minapa, also known as Acintapa, much beloved in Devapala's kingdom, appeared before the dying boy. In response to the prince's pleas for help, Minapa told him that he would offer him instruction that would lead to his healing. Whereupon the yogin gave the prince initiation and empowerment and taught him the yoga of potbellied breathing.

"Upon the successful conclusion of this practice," said Minapa, "your body will once again become whole." And he left the boy under the tree.

Striding across the grassy plain, the guru came upon a group of cowherds within shouting distance of the young victim. How one of them offered to serve the prince is related in the legend of Goraksa.

For a period of twelve years the prince remained in meditation, practicing what his guru had taught him.

The evening before the twelfth anniversary of his wounding, a party of the king's merchants chanced to camp for the night not far from the prince's tree. As the caravan was laden with gold, silver, and precious stones, the merchants feared a midnight raid by bandits. They decided that at the setting of the sun they would take the treasure some distance from the camp and bury it. But when they passed near the royal tree, a voice rang out in the gloom asking, "Who goes there?"

The merchants were terrified. Had they camped near a robbers' den after all? Apprehensively, they called out, "We are only simple charcoal makers."

"So be it," cried the voice.

The next morning, just before sunup, the merchants came to dig up their treasure. But when they examined it to make sure all was well, they were shocked to discover lumps of charcoal instead of ingots and gems.

Fearing for their lives if they returned to the king empty-handed, they discussed what to do. They had nearly decided to separate and flee to the four corners of the earth, when the wisest among them spoke up.

"Remember the voice that called out to us in the night?" he asked. "I believe it must have been a saint whose very words become manifest, a being so pure he can only speak the truth. Let us seek him out. Surely, we have nothing more to lose."

So they retraced their steps and came upon a lone tree under which sat a limbless man. Gathering around him, they recounted their tale of woe and begged for his help.

"Perhaps I spoke in my meditation," said the prince, "and the sound of my voice changed the appearance of your wares. I have no way of knowing. But if I am responsible then let the charcoal once again become gold and silver and precious gems."

Opening the sacks in which they had found charcoal, the merchants shook the contents out upon the ground. There, gleaming in the morning sun, were rubies, diamonds, and sapphires and beautifully wrought items of beaten silver and gold. Awe-stricken, the merchants prostrated themselves before Caurangi and made offerings of their most precious wares.

Quite as astonished as they, the prince suddenly remembered Minapa's words all those long years before. Was this a sign that his practice was finished? Would the prophecy come true? Would his limbs be made new?

All that day he sat in meditation, praying for the restoration of his arms and legs. Slowly, slowly, they began to materialize out of thin air. In a flash, Caurangi realized that just as the earth is the mother of all that grows, so pervasive emptiness was the ground from which sprang his re-membered limbs.

Alas, only the tree had borne witness to Caurangipada's practice. No one else was ever to learn it. Although the prince gained every mundane siddhi and performed innumerable miracles, his irascible temperament kept him from teaching his secrets to others.

Still, it is said that the tree that was his companion for the twelve years of his practice stands in the same spot to this very day.

KANKARIPA
The Lovelorn Widower

My dakini consort, my queen, my lady.
Pure awareness made visible,
Empty space made tangible.
Joined to me yet not part of me,
You are beyond words, beyond compare.

Kankaripa was a man of the common folk, a simple householder of low caste. As was proper for his kind, he married a girl of his own social status and settled down. With the revelations of the conjugal bed, all his energies focused upon the realization of sexual bliss. He became a sensualist who experienced undreamed-of ecstasy. Between these peaks of transport he mused on his happy lot, swearing that this world alone could fulfill all his desires.

But the Wheel of Life turned on its course, and a few years later in the midst of youth and joy, his beloved wife came to her appointed time and died.

Dazed and bewildered, unable to comprehend this lightning stroke of total loss, he carried her body to a cremation ground. There, his mind and will gave way. The corpse in his arms, he collapsed in the ashes, refusing to surrender his beloved to the flames.

A yogin chanced to be passing by. He sat down next to the inconsolable young man and asked, "What is wrong?"

"Rip out my eyes, but give me back my wife," wailed the widower.

"All life ends in death," said the yogin gently, "just as every meeting ends in parting. All compounds disintegrate. Clasping that corpse is no different from clasping a lump of clay. Everyone in this samsaric world suffers. Suffering is the nature of existence. Instead of bewailing your fate, why don't you practice the dharma and rise above pain?"

"My mind is spinning," said the widower. "I can't think clearly. Please help me."

"The guru's instruction is the path to enlightenment," replied the yogin.

"Then please give it to me," cried the young man.

The yogin initiated him and empowered him in the precepts of the insubstantial seed essence that has neither center nor circumference. The heartbroken husband was instructed to meditate upon his wife as a dakini, the emptiness, the indivisible pleasure that has no substance or self.

He spent six years deep in contemplation. As a result all thoughts of his dead wife as a woman of flesh and blood were transformed into a pure state of pleasure and emptiness. As the clear light dawned within, the clouds in his mind dissolved, and he came to see the reality of unalterable truth. In just the way that the datura plant brings its own dreams and hallucinations and takes them away again when it leaves the body, thus did delusion, bewilderment, and unknowing leave his being.

Through such efforts, this ordinary man attained the state of mahamudra-siddhi and became known to the world as Kankaripa, "The Corpse Siddha." During the years before he ascended to the Paradise of the Dakinis, he opened many hearts and minds to the word of the Buddha.

ARYADEVA
The Lotus-Born

All Buddhas—past, present, and future—
Have but a single essence.
To intuit this essence,
Learn the true nature of your own mind.
Then let go and dissolve into unstructured reality.
This tensionless state is the yogin's life.

At birth Aryadeva sprang magically from the pollen-filled heart of a lotus flower. As soon as he came of age, he was ordained in the academy of Sri Nalanda. In time he became the abbot of the famed monastery.

And yet, after a number of years of selfless service, this preceptor of a thousand monks and teacher of countless scholars grew restless. More and more he came to feel that he had not yet realized his own perfect potential. Finally, he resolved to go in search of the guru Nagarjuna, whose extraordinary powers and virtue had inspired his profound respect. In this way he hoped to gain ultimate knowledge.

Believing Nagarjuna to be in the distant south, Aryadeva prepared himself for an arduous journey. However, on the shores of a broad lake not far from Nalanda he chanced to meet a humble fisherman whom he recognized instantly as the Bodhisattva Manjusri. Aryadeva prostrated himself before the great one and presented him with many offerings. When Manjusri offered to grant him a boon in return, the abbot asked if he could tell him the whereabouts of Nagarjuna.

By a stroke of luck the guru he desired was at that very moment in a nearby hermitage in the jungle. According to Manjusri, he was engaged in the formulation of an alchemical potion that would confer immortality.

Setting off in the direction in which the Bodhisattva pointed, it was not long before Aryadeva came upon a humble hut of woven grasses. Nearby he saw a keen-eyed old man muttering to himself as he gathered leaves and roots among the jungle foliage. Aryadeva knew him at once and prostrated himself before the master.

Nagarjuna sensed an extraordinary presence in Aryadeva and wholeheartedly agreed to his new pupil's desire for instruction. He gave him initiation in the mandala of Guhyasamaja and taught him the accompanying precepts. He also agreed to allow Aryadeva to remain with him and practice his sadhana.

Each day the two masters, one the teacher and the other the student, journeyed to a nearby town to beg for food. Nagarjuna had the greatest difficulty getting even the richest householder to give him more than a spoonful of rice. But Aryadeva would come back bearing a veritable feast on the broad back of a banana leaf. Every kind of delicacy imaginable was heaped upon him.

As this went on day after day, Nagarjuna grew cranky and ill-tempered. Finally, he took his student to task. "Lustful women are trying to seduce you with all this fancy cookery," scolded the old man. Throwing the laden banana leaf into the jungle, he said, "This food is unclean. From now on you must eat only what you can lift on the point of a pin."

Aryadeva obeyed his guru faithfully, eating only the single grains of rice he could lift with a pin. But as soon as the women of the town heard of this new stricture, they began preparing cunning little barley cakes covered with syrup and balanced on the point of a pin.

Aryadeva brought these little cakes back to Nagarjuna, who ate them with great relish. But then he grew suspicious once again and asked his pupil where he had received the cakes. In all innocence Aryadeva explained their provenance. The old man flew into a rage and forbade him ever to enter the town again. From now on Nagarjuna would beg for them both.

But the next day, no sooner had the master disappeared from view than a beauteous tree nymph emerged from her leafy home bearing a heavenly feast for Aryadeva. Casually displaying her naked splendor without the slightest hint of embarrassment, she sat down to converse with the lotus-born yogin.

When Nagarjuna returned, his pupil told him about the visit of the tree nymph and gave him the food she had brought. The master decided he had to see this nymph for himself and went to the tree where she lived and called to her. With great modesty she peeped out at him behind a screen of leaves, much too suspicious to show herself.

"Why do you expose yourself to my disciple and not to me?" asked the angry sage.

"I'll tell you why," scolded the tree nymph, "it's because your disciple doesn't even know the meaning of the word 'lust.' He is utterly free and pure. But you, old man, have traces of passion embedded in your aged mind."

Chastened, the guru reflected upon her words. Then he summoned his pupil to him and gave him a new name: Aryadeva, "Sublime God."

That very day Nagarjuna perfected his elixir of eternal youth and annointed his tongue with a few drops. But when he handed the bowl to Aryadeva, his pupil threw the contents against a dead tree, which immediately sprang into full bloom.

"Whatever possessed you to do that!" cried Nagarjuna in dismay. "You're going to have to replace the contents of that bowl."

Obedient as ever, Aryadeva took a bucket of water and peed into it. Then he stirred the contents with a twig and handed it to his guru.

"You've made too much," said the sage peevishly and handed the bucket back to his pupil. Aryadeva splashed half the contents onto another dead tree, and it also was restored to radiant life.

Nodding his head, Nagarjuna said, "It's quite obvious to me that you're already fully realized. Why do you insist on staying in samsara?"

Whereupon, Aryadeva was infused with ecstasy and levitated to the height of seven palm trees. Fully liberated from birth, as are all the lotus-born, he needed only a word from his guru to convince him of what he had been too innocent to see before.

Continuing to float in the sky, he began teaching the Buddha's message to all beings, aiding them to bring their minds to maturity. And when he finished his labors, he turned the soles of his feet to the sky, placed his palms together in adoration, and prostrated himself before his guru. Then, still floating in space, he righted himself. And as the heavenly host gathered to shower flowers down upon him, he simply vanished.

NAGARJUNA
Philosopher and Alchemist

When an unenlightened man pretends to be a siddha
He is like a rebel trying to usurp the king.
When an enlightened man persists in folly
He is like an elephant stuck in the mud.

Many years ago, in Kahora in the eastern kingdom of Kanci, there lived a Brahmin youth of dazzling intellectual powers. By the time he was twenty he could recite from memory all the known Brahmin texts and had even attained the magical gift of invisibility.

But then he grew bored and dissatisfied with his scholarly life; it all seemed empty and sterile to him. And he threw himself headlong into a life of sensual pleasure. Before long there was hardly a household in Kahora he had not plundered of its blossoming maidens and ripe young wives.

Nagarjuna's libertine exploits grew so daring that finally he devised a plan to slip into the king's palace with three friends to have their way with the royal favorites. Alas, they were discovered and pursued. Nagarjuna escaped by standing invisible next to the king himself, but his three friends were beheaded.

The entire district was in an uproar. The Brahmins of Kahora gathered in council to confer about what to do. They discussed this plan and that plan, but in the end they all despaired of finding a way to control the rampaging bull in their midst. Sadly, they decided they would all simply have to emigrate to another district and leave the people to their nemesis.

By this time Nagarjuna himself was caught in a storm of self-disgust. The Brahmins' decision was the final blow.

Everyone breathed a sigh of relief on the day Nagarjuna went willingly, but with much chagrin, into exile. Frustrated and dissatisfied with his life, he set out on a spiritual quest with the same energy he had previously invested in debauchery.

Journeying to the far side of the Cool Garden Cremation Ground, he sought and was given initiation in the doctrine of the Buddha. He next journeyed to the famous monastic academy of Sri Nalanda, where he studied the five arts and sciences until he could recite the academy's entire library from memory.

But ever growing in the center of his being, spiritual dissatisfaction again sent out shoots of unrest. Books were no longer sufficient. And so he began to practice a meditation propitiating Tara, the Savioress. When her face appeared before him in his practice, he abandoned the security of the monastery and took up the life of a mendicant monk.

He traveled far and wide, begging in towns and villages. But still Nagarjuna was not at peace. When he lay down at night, he would think to himself, I am but a worthless wretch. Of what use am I to anyone?

He next decided to go on retreat in Rajagrha. There, he began to propitiate the Elemental Consorts by chanting mantras. He began by propitiating the Twelve consorts of the Supreme Elemental.

On the first day of his retreat an earthquake shook the countryside.

On the second day the river overflowed its banks and there was a vast flood.

On the third day a holocaust of fire descended from the heavens.

On the fourth day a tremendous windstorm blew up.

On the fifth day a shower of spears fell point-first from the sky.

On the sixth day vajra thunderbolts hurtled down.

On the seventh day the Twelve consorts gathered in all their might to attack and overwhelm the meditator. But no matter what they did, they could not distract him even for a fraction of a second. He remained steadfast in his inviolable commitment.

Acknowledging his mastery, the female Elementals drew near him. "Ask, and you shall receive," they said humbly.

"I don't really need anything," Nagarjuna replied. "Except, perhaps, a daily supply of food to sustain me through my retreat."

Each day thereafter, for twelve years, the Elementals brought him four handfuls of rice and five handfuls of vegetables. By the end of his sadhana all one hundred and eight Elemental consorts were under his control.

Renewed and infused with new purpose, Nagarjuna set forth with the clear intention of serving all sentient beings. As his first act he decided to turn Gandhasila Mountain into pure gold. Moving in stages, he first changed the mountain to solid iron. Next, he changed it into gleaming copper.

But just as he was about to transform it into gold, the voice of the Bodhisattva Manjusri rang out. "What makes you think you are aiding all sentient beings by turning this mountain into gold?" asked the divine one. "It will cause great conflict and strife. How do you think you can help mundane beings with gold? It will only provoke greater sin and evil."

Nagarjuna acknowledged the greater wisdom of the Bodhisattva and abandoned the project. To this very day Gandhasila Mountain has a deep coppery color.

Next he traveled far to the south until he came to the banks of a broad river near Sri Parvata Mountain. When he asked some herdsmen to direct him to a safe ford, they led him to the most dangerous part of the river. It was bounded by steep stony banks and infested with crocodiles. Yet the herdsmen insisted it was the safest place to cross.

But just as the yogin was about to step into the water, another herdsman took pity on him and warned him of the great danger. He was a big, burly man with a hearty voice, and Nagarjuna trusted him at once.

"I'll take you to a safe crossing, holy sir," said the herdsman, and he led the yogin to another ford. "Climb up on my shoulders," he said. "I'll get you to the other side, and dry too."

But suddenly, without warning, in the middle of the crossing they were surrounded by ravening crocodiles, thrashing and churning the water into white foam.

"You have nothing to fear as long as I'm alive," shouted the trusty herdsman. And he walked right straight through the melee, landing his passenger safely on the other side.

"Do you recognize me?" asked the yogin, turning to the herdsman. "I am Arya Nagarjuna."

"I have heard of you," replied the herdsman, suddenly overcome with awe.

"You may have whatever your heart desires for carrying me safely across the river," said Nagarjuna, neglecting to mention that it was he who had conjured up the crocodiles as a test.

Without a moment's hesitation, the herdsman replied, "Make me a king."

Whereupon the master splashed some river water against a nearby *sal* tree, and it was immediately transformed into a magnificent white elephant with royal trappings. It bowed low before the new king and assisted him to mount with its trunk.

"How about an army?" the king called down to Nagarjuna.

"When the elephant trumpets, the army will appear, O king," the yogin replied.

Just then the blast of the elephant's call shook the forest, and in the twinkling of an eye, an entire army appeared, magnificently outfitted and armed, ready to march.

In time the herdsman came to be known as King Salabandha. With his wife, Queen Sindhi, he ruled over 8,400,000 households with great wisdom and benevolence.

But he too was infected with the same dissatisfaction that plagued his master. And after a number of years, the herdsman-turned-king went on pilgrimage, searching for his guru. When he found him, he prostrated himself before Nagarjuna and walked around him in propitiating circles for some time before he dared to open up his heart.

"This business of governing isn't anything like I thought it would be," he confessed at last. "It is my heart's desire to renounce my kingdom. Please let me stay here with you from now on."

"No," said Nagarjuna. "I cannot allow you to do that. However, take this Precious Rosary as your preceptor. It will protect you and your kingdom. And I will also give you the divine nectar that confers both immortality and fearlessness in the face of death upon those who taste its honeyed sweetness."

"If you will promise me that a time will come when I can stay here with you always, then I will accept your gifts and return to my kingdom. But if the answer's no, I don't want either of them."

"We shall see," replied Nagarjuna, quashing all his disciple's complaints with instruction on the art of alchemy, the source of the nectar of immortality. And he sent him back to his people for another hundred years.

During that span, Salabandha's kingdom prospered. The harvests were abundant, and all the people and creatures of his realm thrived and multiplied. During these happy years, Nagarjuna spread the teachings of the Buddha from one end of the land to the other.

But in the fullness of time the Wheel of Existence turned once more. Just as it began to appear that this golden age would last forever, the evil spirit known as Sundarananda grew jealous and resentful of the king. He nursed his grievances until his power grew so great that portents of doom appeared in the land. The light and warmth of the sun itself began to diminish, and the face of the blessed moon disappeared from the night sky. Fruit fell from the trees before it was ripe. Rains came at the wrong time, and famine ravaged the land. The fields and forests withered and turned yellow. And an age of sickness and war began.

King Salabandha interpreted these ominous signs to mean that his guru was in mortal danger. Yielding his throne to his eldest son, he traveled with a few of his most faithful servants to sit at the feet of Nagarjuna. When the master asked him why he had come, the king sang him a lament:

> Why has misfortune befallen us?
> Why has the Buddha's doctrine failed us?
> Why are the powers of darkness rising?
> Why have evil storm clouds eclipsed
> The whiteness of the moon, the compassion of Mahakarunika?
> Is my holy guru, the Indestructible Diamond,
> Falling prey to decay and death?
> Evil portents have driven me here.
> I pray you, bestow upon us
> Your compassionate grace.

The master sang to him in reply:

> All birth ends in death.
> All creation ends in dissolution.
> All accumulation ends in dispersion.
> All that appears real is transitory.
> Ignore these omens. Come,
> Drink the elixir of fearlessness!

But no sooner had the last notes of Nagarjuna's song died away than the king's greatest fear came to pass: The guru gave away all his worldly goods and prepared for death. The great god Brahma appeared in the guise of a Brahmin to beg for the master's head. But when Nagarjuna agreed, King Salabandha's heart broke. Grief-stricken, he laid his own head at his guru's feet and died.

The gathered populace cursed the Brahmin for his request. To a man, they all refused to decapitate the master. Eventually, Nagarjuna was forced to take a stalk of *kusa* grass and perform the deed himself. When it was done, the master took his own severed head in his hands and handed it to the Brahmin. All green things withered, and the virtue and merit of men faded from the land. Eight *yaksis,* the female Elementals so faithful to his service, came to stand guard over Nagarjuna's body. And they stand there still.

After the master's death a great light entered the body of Nagabodhi, Nagarjuna's spiritual son and successor. To this very day that light radiates like the beams of a full moon on the clearest of nights. When the teachings and loving-kindness of Maitreya, the Buddha Yet to Come, encompass the earth, Nagarjuna will rise again to serve us all.

VINAPA
The Music Lover

After years of perseverance and devotion
I mastered the vina's errant chords.
Then I found the unstruck sound
And lost my self

Vinapa was the only son of the King of Gauda, a realm bordered by Mother Ganga. He was dearly beloved by his parents and the court. Eight nurses indulged his every whim, and the court musicians came to soothe him whenever he was fretful. Perhaps this early exposure to the deep realms of music changed his fate? For, as the prince grew older, he ignored his lessons in statecraft and pestered the court musicians continually until they agreed to teach him to play the *tambura*.

Hour after hour, day after day, the young prince would pluck the four strings of the tambura. His fingers never seemed to tire of coaxing the deep droning hum, the breath of OM, from his instrument. He was so gifted that he mastered the tambura in a short while, and then he learned to play the seven-stringed *vina*. As he plucked the vina with his plectrum, the additional strings of the instrument would vibrate in perfect sympathy. Entranced by the feminine insightfulness of this instrument, the young prince could not be parted from it. He was obsessed with the vina. He could hardly bear to set it down to take a few morsels of food.

But he was no ordinary musician. He was the heir-apparent to the throne. When the time came, would he be able to rule the kingdom with wisdom and compassion? Would he have the skill, the interest, to do so? His parents and the court grew more and more concerned.

Despairing, they finally summoned a highly trained yogin called Buddhapa

in hopes that he could wean the prince away from music. At their first meeting the young prince was deeply affected by the remarkable qualities of this holy man. Recognizing his master, Vinapa prostrated himself before the yogin and walked around him in reverential circles. Then they sat down to speak deeply, from the heart, about life and death and all that lies between and beyond.

Buddhapa had known instantly that the prince was ready for spiritual training. In the course of their conversation he asked the young man if he was ready to undertake a sadhana, the practice that disciplines the mind on the path to Buddhahood.

"My music is my sadhana, venerable yogin," replied the prince. "Nothing matters to me but my vina and the sound of the tambura. The only sadhana I would practice is one that I could learn without abandoning music."

"If you are as dedicated to music as you say, then I shall teach you a musical sadhana," promised the guru. Whereupon he initiated the prince with the rite that mellows the immature mindstream.

"Meditate continuously upon the sound of your instrument," Buddhapa instructed him. "But while doing so you must free yourself of all distinction between the sound that is struck and what the mind perceives. Cease all mental interference with the sound. Cease all conceptualizing. Cease all critical and judgmental thought. Contemplate only pure sound."

The prince practiced the precepts he had been taught for nine years, during which time he grew to manhood. And as he grew in body he also grew in mind and spirit. All that lay between him and pure cognition was erased from his mind as shadows flee from a clear light. And this very light began to glow within him as though he were a precious butter lamp, and he attained the state of mahamudra-siddhi.

Wondrous were the feats he performed. He could foretell the future, read the thoughts of those around him, and appear in more than one place at the same time. He became universally renowned, and it was said that he had gained his siddhi directly from the deity Hevajra himself.

His true kingdom lay in the realms of spirit. All his long life he taught multitudes of beings how to find release from the bonds of existence. And when he completed his task, he was assumed bodily into the Paradise of the Dakinis.

THAGANAPA
Master of the Lie

To release water in the ear,
Inject water into the ear.
To see truth,
Contemplate all phenomena as a lie.

Thaganapa was born into a low-caste family in eastern India. Early on, he showed criminal tendencies, and in time his entire life and livelihood came to depend upon exploitation and deception.

One day he was sitting on a log at the edge of a town plotting a beautiful con job, when a wise monk chanced to pass by.

"Why are you so deep in thought, my friend?" asked the monk. "It's a long story, venerable sir," Thaganapa began.

But the monk interrupted. "You're about to tell me a lie, aren't you? Haven't you learned that the more you lie, the more you believe lying is normal, and the more your habit of lying will be strengthened. If you continue on this way, when your karma matures, you will be reborn in hell."

Thaganapa turned pale and began to tremble.

"Lying has physical effects as well, you know," the monk went on. "Your tongue gets furrowed, your breath stinks, and your speech becomes ineffectual and unconvincing. A liar's karma makes all fields infertile and the seeds you sow dry and impotent."

Thaganapa had not heard the doctrine of karma applied to lying before, and the monk's apt analysis hit home. "You've seen right through me," he admitted. "They call me Thaganapa because I cannot speak so much as a hundredth part of a hairsbreadth of truth. I lie to everybody—no exception. But what can I do about it?"

"Do you think you're capable of practicing a sadhana?" asked the monk.

"Well, I suppose I could try," said Thaganapa doubtfully. "But I've been lying for so long I don't know if I can stop."

"You're not the only liar since time began," said the monk kindly. "There are precepts even for those such as you."

"All right then," said Thaganapa, relieved. "Go ahead."

The monk began to give Thaganapa instruction in the yoga called "removing water in the ear by means of water"—a meditation that uses deception as an antidote to deception. Next, he gave him the initiation that matures the immature mindstream. And then the monk taught him these precepts: "All that you see, hear, touch, think you perceive with the six senses, indeed, all that you experience, is nothing but a lie."

> Ignorant that all phenomena is a lie,
> You say you are a liar.
> But if knowledge and the knower,
> The six senses and all that is sensed,
> Are lies, then what is truth?
> Childish ignorance of the universal lie
> Holds falseness to be true.
> When we tell ourselves that deception is truth
> We bind ourselves to the round of existence
> Like the liquid drops on the rim of a water wheel.
> Therefore contemplate
> All experience as inherently deceptive,
> All form as inherently deceptive,
> All sound as inherently deceptive.
> In time, you will discover
> That even your belief in deception is a lie.

For seven years Thaganapa meditated upon all perceptual knowledge as deception. At the conclusion of his sadhana, he gained the understanding that all experience of the phenomenal world is a fiction.

Gaining perfect detachment, he came to see all phenomena as dream, hallucination, castles in the air, reflections of the moon in water, images in a mirror. And with his detachment he acquired the qualities of clarity, control, and equanimity. Thinking that he had gained the ultimate goal, he sought out his guru for confirmation.

The monk said simply, "Experience is neither deception nor truth. Reality is uncreated, indeterminate. Now you must meditate upon your experience of all things as emptiness rendered empty by its very nature."

Thaganapa obeyed his guru and returned to his practice. His path was one of resolving paradox, of weaving conflicting thoughts and feelings together into a tapestry of the inherent emptiness of all things.

Gaining siddhi, he was known to all as "Master of the Lie," and he taught those with good karma how to "release water in the ear by means of water." After many years of selfless service, he was assumed into the Paradise of the Dakinis.

CAMARIPA
The Divine Cobbler

I mold the leather of preconception and conceptual thought
Around the last of emptiness and compassion.
Taking the awl of intuitive insight,
I stitch with the thread of existence
That knows no beginning and no end. Spontaneously,
Freed of the eight mundane obsessions,
I create fine slippers of dharmakaya.

In eastern India, in the town of Visnunagar, there lived a humble cobbler. All the day long he worked and worked, making new shoes and repairing old. And as he worked he daydreamed, thinking over and over, "I wasn't meant to be a cobbler all my life."

One day, when he could bear it no longer, he chanced to look up from his work just as a monk was passing by his shop. Throwing down his tools, he dashed out into the street and prostrated himself in the dust at the holy man's feet.

"I am sick and tired of this life of endless toil, passion, and stupidity," he cried. "I have always wanted to follow the Buddha's path but have never had the chance before. Please, venerable sir, teach me something that will benefit me in this world and the next."

The kindly monk raised the cobbler to his feet and said, "If you feel that you are now able to follow a sadhana, then I would be pleased to instruct you."

"Yes, oh, yes," replied the joyous cobbler. "Come and eat with us in our poor outcaste home," he implored.

"I will be there at sundown," said the monk.

The cobbler rushed home to tell his wife and daughters, and the household flew into a whirlwind of activity—cleaning, and cooking, and making the finest preparations their simple means would allow. When the honored guest arrived at the cobbler's hovel, everything was in readiness.

With the greatest respect, the family begged the monk to be seated and washed his feet. The humble feast was served, and their guest took part with great pleasure. Afterward, the cobbler's wife and daughters offered him every comfort, including a soothing massage.

The monk was delighted with this generous welcome and gave both the cobbler and his wife initiation, instructing them thusly:

> Mold the leather of passion and conceptual thought
> Around the last of loving-kindness and compassion.
> Then, taking the guru's precepts as your awl,
> Stitch carefully with the thread
> Of freedom from the eight obsessions.
> Miraculously, you will create those slippers
> That cannot be seen by those with clouded vision—
> The marvelous slippers of dharmakaya.

"Your practice," said the monk, "is to visualize your shoemaking as your meditation."

The cobbler immediately understood the guru's metaphor and asked, "How will I know that I am making progress?"

"At first," said the guru, "you will feel an even stronger revulsion for samsara. But in time, whatever arises will dissolve into its own essential nature." At this, the monk vanished.

The cobbler practiced his sadhana for twelve years, forming out of his meditation the mystical slippers of his guru's instruction. Shod in the dharmakaya, with one step he traversed the ground of ignorance underlying the six passions. All impediments vanished from his mind like smoke, and he attained mahamudra-siddhi.

Visvakarman, the god of arts and crafts, came to the shoemaker's shop attended by his glorious retinue. As the cobbler sat looking on, detached from all worldly things, the god himself took up the tools and leather lying on the workbench and began making shoes.

The people of Visnunagar knew nothing of the cobbler's practice, still less of the degree of his achievement, until one day a new customer came into the shop. There, before his wondering eyes, sat the cobbler lost in meditation while the great god Visvakarman labored in his stead at the bench.

Overnight, the entire town learned of the miracle. One by one, the people came to see for themselves. They prostrated themselves at the feet of the cobbler-yogin and begged him for instruction. He taught them about the indispensable benefits of the guru's instruction and then explained the workings of many different doctrines and techniques.

They gave him the name of Carmaripada, "The Cobbler Siddha," and he was known far and wide for his marvelous deeds. In due time he ascended in his own body to the Paradise of the Dakinis.

SYALIPA
The Jackal Yogin

A gifted artist can blend shape and color
Into such an image of terror,
That gazing at his work we grow afraid.
But look again. Set aside your fear,
And all that remains is but a reflection.

Syalipa was a low-caste laborer from the town of Bighapur. He was so poor that the only hovel he could afford lay right on the edge of the cremation ground. This in itself would not have been so bad, except for one thing. Every night packs of jackals roamed the cremation ground searching among the ashes for bones and bits of unconsumed flesh. True to the nature of their kind, they fought and snarled and howled in the darkness.

Night after night those terrible howls coursed through the poor man's body like bolts of lightning. Night after night he grew more and more afraid. The few hours he managed to sleep were filled with terrible dreams of jackals. He became obsessed with them.

Late one afternoon, a mendicant monk chanced to come to the laborer's shack to beg some food. Syalipa welcomed him in and prostrated himself at the monk's feet. He shared with his guest all that his humble circumstances would allow and chatted about the news of the town.

The monk was very appreciative of his host's kind attentions and began to explain to Syalipa the kind of rewards that generosity attracted. The laborer was very interested and tried to listen with all his mind. But night had fallen, and his every nerve was strained awaiting that first bloodcurdling howl from the cremation ground.

Soon the night resounded with howls, and the monk could not help but notice his host's ashy pallor and hollow eyes. "What are you afraid of?" he asked. "Do you fear the suffering of the round of existence? After all, what else is there to fear but life, death, and rebirth?"

"We all fear samsara, holy one," replied Syalipa. "But I have another fear. Listen . . ."

The monk listened quietly for a moment, and then said, "I hear only the songs of jackals on the cremation ground, nothing more."

"Nothing more!" cried Syalipa. "That's quite enough. I'm terrified of those howls. Every night I lie awake trembling with fear of jackals."

"Ah, now I understand," said the kindly monk. "I have precepts and a mantra that can help you. But first I think you should take initiation."

Syalipa was so grateful that he offered the pittance he had been able to save as the initiation fee. Whereupon the monk gave him empowerment and instructed him in the practice called "the fear that destroys fear."

"The antidote for the one thing in life that you fear lies in discovering the true nature of that fear," said the monk. "Now, this is what you must do. Build a hut in the very middle of the cremation ground where you will be one with the jackals themselves. There, you must meditate upon the jackals' howls as the root of all sound. You must come to hear no difference between the howls and any other sound."

Terrifying as the monk's counsel seemed, Syalipa obeyed. Gradually, he came to hear the silence at the heart of all sound. As he grew more and more detached from his fear, he came to recognize the jackals' howls as the union of sound and emptiness. Meditating upon the cause of his terror became a self-liberating experience of fearless pleasure.

After practicing his sadhana for nine years, all the defilements of his mind and body disappeared like fading echoes, and he attained mahamudra-siddhi.

Donning a jackal skin as a symbol of his ability to taste the one flavor of all things, he came to be called, "The Jackal Yogin." For many years he taught his innumerable disciples the practices concerning the oneness of appearances and emptiness. Finally, he rose bodily into the Paradise of the Dakinis.

NAROPA
The Dauntless Disciple

As the hosts of the Universal Emperor
Conquer all the continents and the many islands,
So the yogin who knows the taste of sahaja, the Innate,
Conquers samsara, and pure pleasure reigns.

Naropa came from Pataliputra, of mixed-caste parentage. His father was a liquor seller, but when the time came to follow his father's profession, Naropa rejected it and went into the forest to become a wood gatherer. Even there his restless, seeking soul gave him no rest.

One evening he chanced to hear tales of the great sage Tilopa. Then and there he decided that Tilopa was his guru and he would not rest until he had found him. The next day he traded a load of wood to a hunter for the yogin's traditional deerskin and set off toward Visnunagar in search of his master.

When he reached his destination he was dismayed to learn that the great sage had recently left and no one knew where he might be. Undaunted, Naropa set off on a journey that was to last for years and take him the length and breadth of India, as he followed every hint, every whisper of where Tilopa might be.

One day, when the dust sat heavy in the windless air, Naropa was on the road to nowhere in particular when he chanced to see a figure approaching in the hazy distance. For no discernible reason his heart leaped in his throat. As if they had a mind of their own, his feet flew down the road toward the as yet unrecognizable figure.

But the closer he came the surer he grew. And finally, when he could make out the face and form of the other traveler, he knew. He had found Tilopa at last. He flew to the master's side, prostrated himself in the dust at his feet, then began dancing circles about him, addressing him as "guru" and inquiring after his health.

Tilopa stopped still in the middle of the road, fixed Naropa with an angry stare and shouted: ""Stop all this nonsense. I am not your guru. You are not my disciple. I have never seen you before and hope never to lay eyes on you again!" Then he thrashed Naropa soundly with his stout walking stick and told him to get out of his way.

But Naropa was neither surprised nor discouraged. Now that he had found the master he had sought for so many years, his faith was certainly not going to be shaken by a few blows. He simply set off for the nearest town to beg food for them both.

When he returned, Tilopa ate heartily without so much as a word of greeting and beat him soundly once again. Silent, Naropa contented himself with the leftover scraps and once again walked around and around his guru in reverential circles.

For twelve long years he remained by Tilopa's side, begging food and serving him in all things. Not once did he receive a kind word. Not once did Tilopa acknowledge him as his pupil. And not once did Naropa's faith waver.

Toward the end of the twelfth year they chanced upon a village celebrating feast of a wealthy man's daughter. The generous host had provided the guests with eighty-four different types of curry. One of the dishes was rare and so exquisite that one taste would make you believe you had dined with the gods.

Naropa was given large helpings of all the curries, including the great delicacy. When he returned to Tilopa and spread out the feast, an amazing thing happened: for the first time in all the years Naropa had known him, Tilopa smiled. Then he helped himself to every morsel of the special dish. Licking his fingers, he handed Naropa his empty bowl, asking, "Where did you find this, my son? Please return and fetch me some more."

"'My son'! He called me 'my son'!" thought Naropa, happy as a Bodhisattva on the first level of the path. "For twelve years I have sat at my guru's feet without so much as being asked my name. And now he has called me 'my son'!" Floating in ecstasy, he returned to the wedding feast to ask for more of the special curry for his master.

Naropa's dakini, Vajra Yogini (opposite)

But such was Tilopa's appetite that he sent his disciple back again and again. Each time, to Naropa's great relief, he was given more of the elegant dish. But when Tilopa sent him back yet a fifth time, Naropa was ashamed to show his face, and a great inner struggle raged within him. Finally, unable to face his guru's displeasure, he made up his mind to steal the entire pot.

Waiting for the right moment, he lingered on the fringes of the crowd, edging slowly toward the pot of curry. And as soon as all the guests and servants were occupied with some ceremonial occurrence, he abandoned his self-respect, snatched up the pot, hid it under his robes, and made his getaway.

Tilopa praised him for lowering himself to such a level of humiliation, further commending him for all his years of perseverance. Calling him "my diligent son," Tilopa then bestowed the initiation and blessing of Vajra Varahi upon him and gave him instruction in meditation.

Within six months Naropa gained mahamudra-siddhi, and a light began to flow from his being so intensely that it could be seen as far as a month's journey from his hermitage. His fame spread like wildfire, and devotees flocked to him from the four quarters of the world.

After years of tireless devotion to his countless disciples, he was assumed bodily into the Paradise of the Dakinis.

TILOPA
The Great Renunciate

The bird that alights on the cliffs of Mount Meru
Appears to be made of pure gold.
The sage who realizes that all is pure potential
Flies from the material world
And alights in the Buddha-fields of Bliss.

For many years Tilopa performed priestly duties in the service of the king of Visnunagar. Grateful for the great sage's efforts in teaching the Buddha's doctrines to innumerable disciples, the king rewarded him with the princely sum of five hundred gold sovereigns a day.

And yet, despite the success of his work and the gracious bounty of his life, Tilopa was very uneasy in his mind and distracted in his work. "My life is meaningless," he thought to himself. "There is some essential teaching for which my soul longs that I cannot discover in these luxurious surroundings. I must leave and seek enlightenment by living as a yogin."

But whenever Tilopa attempted to resign, such a cry of dismay and loss rose from his disciples, and from the court and the royal family, that each time the king refused him permission to leave.

Finally, one night, Tilopa's longing became so intense that he knew, come what may, he could no longer remain. Leaving a brief note that read, "I will never return. Do not attempt to follow me," he silently made his way to the temple. There he sought out a beggar, exchanged his priestly robes for the poor man's rags, and slipped unnoticed out of the royal compound.

By dawn Tilopa was well on the road to Kanci, where he took up residence on the cremation ground. He lived there quietly for a time, practicing his

sadhana and begging for food in the town. Later on he resumed his mendicant roaming. One day on the road he met Naropa, who became his faithful and devoted servant.

After many years of practicing his sadhana, the defilements that had so troubled Tilopa's mind simply vanished. He attained mahamudra-siddhi and was himself honored and served sumptuously in the paradise of the gods. He acquired the siddhis of Body, Speech, and Mind, and became universally renowned. After setting innumerable beings on the path of enlightenment, he ascended to the Paradise of the Dakinis.

SANTIPA
The Academic

Just as a child nourished by its mother
Grows into the strength of adulthood,
So an immature mind nourished by the guru's precepts
Grows into the bliss of the mahayana.
Just as disease is cured by a doctor's medicines,
So the malaise caused by belief in "I" and "mine"
Is cured instantly by the guru's instruction.

When King Devapala ruled Magadha, the monk Santipa, a renowned preceptor also known as Ratnakarasanti, and who was by birth a Brahmin, became celebrated as a teacher of the five arts and sciences at the famed monastic academy of Vikramasila. His fame spread as far as Sri Lanka, where King Kapina, a man of virtue and merit, had become interested in the Buddha's doctrine. Hungry to learn more, the king and his court decided the great sage Santipa must become their guru.

This was how a royal messenger bearing gifts of great worth happened to arrive at the gates of the monastery. Prostrating himself before the great teacher, he spoke in the words of the king. "I bring you gold and silver, pearls and fine silks, carvings of teak and ivory, spices and rare herbs. These are but a small token of the profound respect in which you are held by King Kapina and all the people of Sri Lanka. Take pity on us, great sage. We are but barbarians who live in darkness and ignorance, consumed by the fires of lust and greed, tortured by the weapons of anger and hatred. Come to us. Spread the liberating message of the mahayana—the great approach to Buddhahood—for we know it not. Come to the island of Sri Lanka for the sake of its people."

After some reflection, Santipa decided it was his duty to go. He took sail with an entourage of two thousand monks and innumerable oxen and horses loaded with the tripitaka—the three "baskets" of scripture.

When the people of Sri Lanka learned of their imminent arrival, they were as happy as Bodhisattvas on the first level of the tenfold path. One by one they left their work to gather on the beach. At the sight of the first sail, their hearts leapt with joy. When the boats crowded with canopies and oxen appeared over the horizon, they were ecstatic.

They spread the ground with silk for the great preceptor to walk upon; and all bowed low in homage as he stepped foot upon their land. He was sur-rounded with clouds of rare incense, and flowers were heaped upon him, and his party. The king's servants hurried to fulfill his every need.

The great teacher remained in Sri Lanka for three years, imparting the many doctrines and techniques of the tripitaka to the king, his court, and his people.

Santipa's leaving was as splendid as his arrival. The grateful monarch gave him thousands of horses and oxen, as well as precious artifacts of gold and sil-ver, and the darkest of coral that came only from great depths in the sea. On the return voyage, the sage decided to take the longer route home. After the ocean crossing, the party journeyed through the kingdom of Ramesvaram, where King Ramana had built a great temple to Mahadeva in gratitude for the recovery of his wife from Lankapuri in Sri Lanka.

Finally, all that lay between them and home was a seven-day journey across a barren plateau surrounded by forbidding mountains. It was on the fourth day of this trek that Santipa encountered Kotalipa, a peasant who became his dis-ciple and whose story is recounted later in this book.

After the return to the monastery, life soon returned to normal. Santipa resumed his studies and teaching. Time passed and Santipa began to grow old and infirm. His students took to driving him around in a buffalo cart, and they fed him upon sweetmeats and other soft foods because he had lost his teeth. When he reached his one-hundredth birthday, he retired from active life and began a twelve-year period of contemplation.

However, during those same twelve years, on the barren plain Santipa had traversed on his return from Sri Lanka, the peasant Kotalipa was also in retreat. While Santipa was practicing discursive contemplation, Kotalipa was absorbed in the essential nature of reality, and his nondiscursive, thought-free meditation led directly to mahamudra-siddhi.

In time, Santipa returned from his retreat and was much acclaimed by his students.

When Kotalipa attained mahamudra-siddhi, Indra, lord of the gods, came to celebrate. Surrounded by numerous dakinis and his divine entourage, the great god poured ambrosia into "the gate of purity," the crown cakra on top of Kotalipa's head. This infused the yogin with complete contentment. The dakinis cried: "This is the real Vajrasattva," and Kotalipa blessed them, which filled them with divine happiness. Throughout the festivities, Kotalipa kept insisting, "It was my guru's instruction that helped me attain siddhi. I was plowing the mountainside, but he taught me to plow the mind."

Indra and his hosts invited Kotalipa to enter the Thirty-three Sensual Paradises, but the yogin could think only of his guru. He refused, saying, "Is not my guru a source of greater grace than the Buddha? Is it not written in the scriptures: 'The guru is the buddha; the guru is the dharma, the guru is the community. The guru embodies the Three Jewels, and I crave his sacred blessings.'"

In his invisible awareness body, Kotalipa transported himself into the presence of Santipa and prostrated himself before the great guru and his entourage. But no one could see him, not even his teacher, so he materialized his physical body and repeated his homage.

"Who are you?" asked Santipa, startled.

"I am your disciple," replied Kotalipa with humble adoration.

Santipa sighed and said, "I'm afraid there have been so many of them that I can't remember them all."

"Don't you remember the peasant you found plowing the mountainside?" asked Kotalipa.

Santipa smiled, for now he recalled the very incident. "What results have you obtained from your meditation?" he asked kindly.

"Following your instructions brought me mahamudra-siddhi and the existential mode of pure awareness and emptiness—the dharmakaya," replied Kotalipa.

Whereupon a great awareness dawned on Santipa. He realized that during all those years of teaching he had neglected true spiritual discipline. "I have a confession to make," he said to his pupil. "I have never experienced the perfect reality that I teach. I have even forgotten the instructions I gave you." He asked his student to demonstrate the results of his meditation.

Thus it was that student became teacher, and teacher became student. Kotalipa took Santipa to a solitary retreat and revealed to him the many qualities of the dharmakaya, thus returning the gift of instruction.

Santipa spent another twelve years in meditation, and then, at long last, he attained mahamudra-siddhi. With the attainment of true bliss, he realized that all his book learning and all the honors and gifts heaped upon him were hollow and trivial by compare. The years remaining to him he spent in faithful service to others. In the end, he too gained the Paradise of the Dakinis.

MEKOPA
The Wild-Eyed Guru

Above all else
The guru would have you realize
The nature of mind.
Then treating all events the same,
Accustoming yourself to non-duality
Live in a cremation ground.
What does it matter that the world
Sees you as a mad saint?

Mekopa was a food seller who lived in a small town in Bengal. He always had a cheerful word for his patrons, and such was his good-heartedness that he often fed the poor for free. This did not escape the notice of a certain yogin whom Mekopa also fed each and every day without asking for the slightest recompense.

"Why are you so generous?" the yogin asked Mekopa one day.

Mekopa laughed and said, "Perhaps I'm storing up merit for a better rebirth."

"If that is truly your wish," said the yogin, "why not let me instruct you in a sadhana that will guarantee you such an outcome."

Mekopa was delighted and promised to practice faithfully what he was taught. The yogin gave him the initiation that transfers grace and instructed him in the nature of mind by reciting these verses:

Your mind is like a magical gem
Manifesting all that is—

From samsara to nirvana.
Since knowing and unknowing form a duality,
Gaze deep into the changeless space
Of mind's true nature
And discover the source of all duality;
Nondual space is without substance,
Thus all experience is an illusion.
Discover how we are bound by delusive desire.

In Mekopa's meditation, he came to realize the truth of his guru's words: that all phenomena are figments of the mind's workings; that the mind itself is vastness without end, where there is neither coming nor going. For six months he remained within the realization of the nature of his own mind.

However, this incredibly intense direct contact with profound truth caused him to roam about the cremation ground like a madman. Often, he would run into town and stare deeply into stranger's eyes with a wild-eyed gaze that pierced the phenomenal world. People began calling him Guru Crazy Eyes. His profound teachings changed many lives, and in time he rose bodily into the Paradise of the Dakinis.

KAMBALA
The Yogin of the Black Blanket

Within the ocean's silent depths
Lies treasure untold—
How marvelous the enjoyment of the Naga kings.
Within all light and all sound
Lies the dharmakaya—
How rich the enjoyment of the adept.

After his father's death, the new king of Kankarama assumed the throne. He then sent for his mother to ask for her wise counsel, but she was nowhere to be found. They searched the palace high and low to no avail. She had simply disappeared.

Despite the weight of his double loss, the king was forced to turn his thoughts to the management of his kingdom. And within a short time his virtue and wisdom had brought great prosperity to the eighty-four thousand households of his realm.

Then, after two years had passed, the queen mother suddenly reappeared at court. Her son was overjoyed as she approached the throne. But when he saw the tears in her eyes, his joy turned to sadness.

"Beloved mother, why are you crying?" asked the king.

"I weep to see you sitting on this throne, engaging in the wretched business of government," she replied.

The young king rose from the throne, removed the crown from his head, and embraced his mother. "Then I will abdicate in favor of my brother and take holy orders," he declared, for his only thought was to please her.

Within the week he took up residence in a monastery, accompanied by a retinue of three hundred monks. After a time, his mother appeared to him again. And again she was weeping. He prostrated himself before her and begged her to explain the cause of her distress.

"Even though you have become a monk, I weep to see you still living like a king surrounded by a court."

"What would you have me do?" he asked.

"Leave this monastery and all its luxury," she said. "Leave your retinue of monks, and go into the jungle alone and meditate."

Once more he followed her instructions. He went into the jungle and took up residence in the shelter of a sturdy tree. However, the local villagers soon became aware of his presence. Grateful for his past generosity, they fed him the finest foods and supplied many things for his comfort.

Once again his mother appeared before him, beating her breast and weeping violently. And once again, the yogin-king begged to know the cause of her displeasure.

Pointing to his silk robes and silver hand basin, she said sternly, "What need has a holy man for all these trappings?"

Abandoning his luxurious jungle retreat and the tender care of his subjects, he took the path of the yogin, wandering from land to land.

Before he had gone far, his mother appeared yet again. However, this time she was floating above him in midair, and he recognized at last her true dakini nature. She gave him the Samvara initiation and instructed him in meditation. Then she vanished from sight.

The yogin-king wandered from place to place for twelve years. He slept in cremation grounds and practiced his sadhana until he attained mahamudra-siddhi. He levitated into the sky, and there he found himself face to face with his mother and all her heavenly retinue. "Why are you indulging your power in this useless fashion?" she asked angrily, her eyes still swollen from weeping. "Why are you not using your gifts for the benefit of those below?"

The master floated back down to earth and, intent upon selfless service, traveled to Mangalapur, the capital of Oddiyana, which lay in the realm of the dakinis. Outside the city of 250,000 households, in the area of Karabir, he came upon the wild and lonely Panaba cliffs. In the cliff wall he found a cave, and this became his retreat. In time, it came to be called Talatse, "Palm-Top Cave."

However, once he took up residence, some new and much less benevolent female elements entered his life. It seems his presence threatened the power of a band of local dakini witches and their queen, Padmadevi. In council they decided to launch a campaign that would interfere with his meditation and make his life so miserable he would be forced to move on.

One day, dressed in the black blanket that was his sole covering, he set out for town to beg food. On the road he was accosted by a bevy of the beautiful young witches.

"Please come home with us," they cried imploringly. "We'd be so honored to feed you. That way you wouldn't have to go all the way to town."

"It's not my custom to take my food from only one household," he replied politely.

"Well, if you won't come home with us," Padmadevi wheedled, "will you lend us your blanket while you're gone?"

Too kindly to refuse her request, he gave her the blanket and, totally naked, continued on into town.

As soon as he had disappeared over the hill, the witches began to laugh with glee and dance madly about with the yogin's blanket. Then Padmadevi called another council.

"The siddha is a man of power," she said, "therefore all his possessions must also partake of his power. How shall we share it between us?" They decided that they must eat the blanket then and there, and they began to tear it into tiny bits. In a trice they had consumed it all—with the exception of one corner, which they threw into the fire.

On his way home from town, the master inquired politely if he might have his blanket back. The witches, of course, could not do this, so they offered him a beautiful new blanket instead. But no, this would not do. The yogin insisted upon having his very own blanket. They tried offering him gold. Again he refused.

Furious, he returned to town to complain to the king. Recounting the tale of his lost blanket, he insisted that the king force the thieving witches to return his property.

The king summoned the witches and demanded that they give the yogin back his blanket. They pleaded that it was no longer in their possession and that they had offered the yogin compensation for it, which he had refused.

What more could the king do? The blanket was simply not to be had. Naked, the master returned to his cave to continue his meditation. There he offered a *torma,* a sacrificial cake, to the dakini Vajra Yarahi, consort of Heruka, to propitiate the elemental spirits. Later, when one of the witches cast a spell that caused the spring in his cave to dry up, he was able to command the earth goddess to restore it. Instantly, fresh sweet water bubbled forth from his spring.

On and on went the petty annoyances. But the master was unconcerned and always managed to set right whatever mischief the witches conjured up. Frustrated, his tormentors decided to hold a great congress of dakini witches in hopes that their concerted power would defeat the master. Witches came from as far away as Mt. Meru and the four continents to the great convocation in Oddiyana.

But the master got wind of what was going on, and he hatched a counterplot of his own. Waiting until they had all gathered about their queen, Padmadevi, he chanted a very powerful mantra that turned them into the least harmful form he could devise—a flock of sheep.

Bleating piteously, Padmadevi entreated him to return them to their original shapes. He agreed but took the precaution of shearing them all first. When the witches returned to their human forms they discovered their heads had been shaved bald. Once more the master found himself in a storm of feminine weeping.

Infuriated at this insult to her power, the Goddess of Sensuality struck another blow for her side. Casting one of her strongest spells, she called up a great wind that dislodged an enormous boulder from the top of the cliffs and sent it hurtling down upon Palm-Top Cave. The master surveyed the oncoming monolith with great calm, and when it was nearly upon him he simply raised his hand in a gesture of warning.

Instantly, the huge rock came to a halt, balancing precariously on an outcropping just above the entrance to his cave. It remains there to this very day.

The war between the master and the witches had brought the business of the kingdom to a halt. No one felt safe, for who knew what would happen next—perhaps a great earthquake or a flood, perhaps fire would rain from the sky? Finally, the king decided to put an end to this disturbance, and he summoned both the master and Padmadevi's troublemaking witches to his court.

Stern and majestic upon his throne, the king observed the witches in silence for some time. At last, he said, "There is not one among you who has not harmed at least one of my male subjects at some time or another. You must now beg forgiveness and vow to follow the path of virtue."

The witches simply laughed at him and remained totally unrepentant. But then, the master, in a voice like thunder, hurled this imprecation at the gathering: "Vow to protect the truth or I will send you this very instant to Dharmaraja, Lord of Death."

In fear and trembling, the witches vowed to do as they were told. Fixing them with his piercing gaze, the master warned: "Should any of you contemplate breaking your vow in even the smallest of infractions, you will be transformed upon the instant into a cart horse."

Knowing the master was as good as his word, the witches took refuge in the Buddha, swearing to abide by his precepts. When they were given a ceremony of purification they all vomited up scraps of the master's blanket that they had consumed. Happy to have his one piece of clothing returned to him, he gathered up all the scraps and sewed them back together again—except, of course, for one small corner. For the piece that had been thrown into the fire was gone forever.

This great yogin became known far and wide as Kambala, "Master of the Blanket," and also as Sri Prabhat, "Glorious Light." After many peaceful years of selfless service to humanity, he was assumed bodily into the Paradise of the Dakinis.

VYALIPA
The Courtesan's Alchemist

There is supreme solitude
In contemplating all-embracing space
And perfect harmony
In realizing the nature of every experience.
But the vision of ultimate reality
Is a vision of your peerless guru.
Only then can you quaff the elixir of immortality
And be truly alive.

Vyali, a very wealthy Brahmin, coveted immortality. And thus he began to practice alchemy in order to discover the secret of the elixir of life. At great expense he acquired a certain rare alchemical manual and purchased a large quantity of quicksilver and rare herbs called for by the formula listed in the book.

He prepared the elixir carefully according to the complex steps outlined in his manual, but in the end he was unable to obtain one crucial ingredient—and after all that time, expense, and care, the potion was worthless. In a fury, he hurled the book into Mother Ganga and in the thirteenth year of his sadhana became a penniless wandering beggar.

Following the course of the river, he found himself in a small village not far from a temple of Ramacandra. There, while begging his food, he chanced to meet a courtesan. During their conversation she told him of a curious thing that had happened to her that day while bathing in the river. A book bobbing on the face of the waters had floated right into her hand—and what a strange book it was. The courtesan showed her treasure to the yogin, who peered at it closely and then laughed like a madman. With tears rolling down his cheeks, he told her the story of his life, for this was the very same alchemical manual that he had thrown into the river himself.

A courtesan's career is as fragile and evanescent as her beauty; and her beauty is as long-lived as her youth. She was very interested in the elixir of life and begged the yogin to take up his work once more, offering him thirty pounds of gold as an incentive.

The gold spoke louder than his disenchantment, and he accepted her offer. Once again he purchased a large amount of quicksilver and labored at his alchemical sadhana for another year with no sign of success. His potion was still missing one crucial ingredient, red myrobalan, a fruit much like the cherry plum, whose restorative properties are much prized in Eastern medicine.

One day, toward the end of the year, the courtesan was taking her daily bath in Mother Ganga when another miraculous event took place. A beautiful red flower came floating down the river and wrapped itself around one of her fingers. She didn't notice it until sometime after she had returned home and was checking on her partner's progress. When she shook the flower off her finger, a drop of nectar fell into the potion and the air was filled with miraculous signs: A wheel of eight auspicious symbols spinning clockwise appeared in the sky over their heads: a precious canopy, two golden fishes, a treasure pot, a *kamala* flower, a white conch shell, an eternal knot, a victory banner, and an eight-spoked wheel.

Vyali's eyes shone with greedy delight. His only concern was whether the courtesan had told anyone else of their experiments. She assured him that she had not.

That evening she decided to test her partner for one more sign of success— she was, after all, a cautious woman. Secretly, she sprinkled another restorative herb, *chiraita* on Vyali's food. It was an exceedingly bitter herb, and until now Vyali had not been able to tolerate it. This time he noticed nothing at all. The courtesan was beside herself with delight.

First, they tried some of the potion out on an aged mare the courtesan had put out to pasture. The creature soon began kicking up her heels and acting very much like the frisky filly she had been in her youth.

Encouraged, Vyali and the courtesan toasted each other's eternal life and partook of the potion. Instantly both achieved mundane siddhi and the power of deathlessness. Even this did not change the selfish, covetous nature of the yogin, and Vyali decided they must keep the secret entirely to themselves, denying it to all other beings.

So selfish was this action that when they ascended into the heavens, the gods spurned them. And so the two immortals went to live in the land of Kilampara. They made their home in the shade of a lone tree on top of a rock one mile high—ten times the distance sound will travel—the whole entirely surrounded by an impenetrable swamp.

But Arya Nagarjuna had achieved the power of flight. And he vowed to recover the secret of immortality, which had been stolen from all mankind. Cleverly, he removed one of his shoes before taking to the air. When he arrived at the top of the rock, he prostrated himself before the mortal pair. They were quite startled to see him and much covetous of his miraculous power of flight. How rich their lives would be if they could go anywhere in the world they desired.

When they questioned Nagarjuna about his remarkable gift, he told them the secret resided in the power of the one shoe he was wearing. After some stiff bargaining, Vyali offered to trade him the recipe for the elixir of life for that remarkable shoe.

Vyali and the courtesan remain on that rock to this very day, for the secret of flight has eluded them still. Without purification of the mind in the practice of sadhana, all the elixirs in the world will still lack the one true ingredient—the penitence and contrition that opens the mindstream to the guru's instruction.

But Arya Nagarjuna returned to India with the precious formula. To this very day he continues his practice for the sake of all sentient beings on top of Sri Parvata Mountain. And to those who find the path to realization, he grants the secret of the magic elixir of life.

TANTEPA
The Gambler

All the workings of my mind have
Dissolved into thought-free space.
Every fleeting experience of phenomena has been
Absorbed in the continuum of emptiness.

Tantepa was a man of low caste who came from Kausambhi, in the valley of Mother Ganga. He gambled compulsively day and night. For him, life was simply a matter of winning or losing, of beating the odds. Most of the time he just managed to break even. But then he hit a fateful losing streak.

He gambled everything and lost everything. But even this didn't stop him; he continued to gamble on credit. Still he lost, and his creditors began getting nasty. When he couldn't come up with the money, he started running and hiding. But there was nowhere left to go. Finally, one day, hungry, penniless, and exhausted, his luck totally ran out. His creditors discovered his hiding place and beat him half to death.

At nightfall Tantepa managed to crawl away to a cremation ground to hide in the shadows and ashes. There, by chance, a yogin discovered him and offered to share his meal.

"Those are pretty bad scrapes and bruises you've got there," said the yogin. "Were you set upon by robbers?"

"I robbed myself, holy sir," said Tantepa. "I'm a gambler. I've gambled away all I owned, and my creditors nearly killed me for welshing on my markers."

"Since nothing else in your life is paying off, why not try meditation?" asked the yogin.

"What are the odds that it'll work?" asked the gambler. Then he burst into tears. "You see!" he sobbed. "That's how I am. For me it all comes down to dots on the dice. I'll tell you one thing, though," he said, brightening. "If you've got a meditation that I could practice without having to give up gambling, I might just try it."

The yogin smiled and said, "Well, young man, you're in luck. It just so happens that I know exactly the right practice for one such as you."

Whereupon he gave the gambler initiation and empowerment. And then he told him: "Now, what you must do is visualize the three realms. These are sensual experience, aesthetic form, and formlessness. You're already familiar with the last one, it's as empty as your pocket is now."

The gambler nodded and smiled wryly. The yogin continued: "After you have visualized the three realms, you must begin to see the nature of your mind as that very same emptiness." And he sang him this song:

> Just as you lost all your money at dice,
> So you must lose all thought of the three realms.
> Just as your creditors smashed you to a pulp,
> So must you smash all the workings of your mind
> Into the emptiness of thought-free space.
> Then this cremation ground will be transformed
> Into the realm of pure pleasure.

Tantepa meditated diligently on his guru's instructions. And as he did, all of his thoughts and beliefs about the nature of the three realms dissolved into the true reality of their own empty spaciousness.

He became a teacher renowned for his compassion and insight into the foibles and failings of his fellow humans. The very last song he sang to his disciples was:

> Had I not known sorrow and remorse,
> How could I have entered the path to release?
> Had I not placed my trust in a teacher,
> How could I have attained the ultimate power?

Scarcely had these words left his lips than he levitated to the height of seven palm trees and entered the Paradise of the Dakinis.

KUKKURIPA
The Dog Lover

Where conscious effort and striving are present
The Buddha is absent,
Thus, ritual and offerings are futile.
Within the peak experience of the guru's grace
The Buddha is present,
But will the fortunate recipient see it?

In Kapilavastu there lived a Brahmin named Kukkuripa. Puzzling over the problems of existence, he came to place his trust in the Tantra and in time chose the path of renunciation. He began his itinerant career by begging his way slowly toward the caves of Lumbini.

One day, on the road to the next town, he heard a soft whining in the underbrush. When he investigated, he found a young dog so starved she could no longer stand. Moved to pity, he picked her up and carried her with him on his long journey, sharing the contents of his begging bowl, and watching with delight as she began to grow strong and healthy.

By the time they arrived in Lumbini, Kukkuripa had become so accustomed to her affectionate, good-natured company that he could not imagine living without her. And so he searched for an empty cave large enough for them both. Every day, when he went out begging, she would stand guard, waiting patiently for his return.

So deeply involved was Kukkuripa in the continuous recitation of his mantra that twelve years passed as quickly as one. Almost without realizing it, the yogin attained the magical powers of prescience and divine insight. But the gods of the Thirty-three Sensual Heavens had taken notice. In fact, they were so

impressed that they invited him to celebrate his achievements by visiting their paradise. Flattered, and amazed at their attentions, he accepted the invitation and embarked upon a ceaseless round of self-indulgent feasting and pleasure.

On earth his faithful dog waited patiently for her master to return. Although she had to root around for whatever she could find to eat, she never strayed far from the cave. And in truth, she was not forgotten. Despite his luxurious existence, Kukkuripa sorely missed his loving companion. Again and again he told the gods that he needed to return to the cave to care for her.

But his heavenly hosts urged him to stay, saying: "How can you even think about returning to a dog in a dark cave when you are enjoying our good favor and every luxury and comfort we can offer? Don't be so foolish—remain with us here." Time and time again, Kukkuripa allowed himself to be persuaded.

But one day when he looked down from the Thirty-three Heavens, he realized that his loyal dog was pining for him—her eyes were sad, her tail drooped, and she was so thin he could see her ribs. Kukkuripa's heart ached for her. Then and there he descended from paradise to rejoin her in the cave.

The dog leaped and pranced with joy when she caught sight of her beloved master. But no sooner did he sit down and begin to scratch her favorite spot behind the ears than she vanished from sight! There before him, wreathed in a cloud of glory, stood a radiantly beautiful dakini.

"Well done!" she cried. "Well done! You have proved your worth by overcoming temptation. Now that you have returned, supreme power is yours. You have learned that the mundane power of the gods is delusory, for they still retain the notion of self. Theirs is the realm of fallible pleasure. But now your dakini can grant you supreme realization—immaculate pleasure without end."

Then she taught him how to achieve the symbolic union of skillful means and perfect insight. As an irreversible, infallible vision of immutability arose in his mindstream, he did indeed attain the state of supreme realization.

Renowned as Guru Kukkuripa, the Dog Lover, he returned to Kapilavastu, where he lived a long life of selfless service. And in due time, he ascended to the Paradise of the Dakinis with a vast entourage of disciples.

KANHAPA
The Dark-Skinned One

No more than you can drive a chariot without wheels
Can the practice of generosity and moral conduct—
Without a guru—gain you siddhi supreme.
As the innately skilled wide-winged vulture
Soars in the heavens above,
So the guru's potent precepts
Instinctively absorbed,
Give the yogin total contentment.

Kanhapa was the son of a scribe. He showed early promise and took ordination in the great monastic academy of Somapuri. There, he was initiated into the mandala of the deity Hevajra by his guru Jalandhara.

After twelve years of practicing his sadhana, the scribe's son was rewarded with a vision of Hevajra and all his heavenly retinue, and the earth trembled under his feet. Inflated with pride, Kanhapa was certain he had attained the ultimate goal. But no sooner had he begun to feel totally pleased with himself than a scolding dakini appeared and warned him that his vision was simply part of the preliminaries. Chastened, Kanhapa continued his solitary practice.

Yet he still could not resist testing out his achievements from time to time. One day he placed his foot gently upon a granite boulder. When he raised it again, he found that he had left his footprint in the hard stone. Once more the scolding dakini returned, and once more she sent him back to his meditation.

The third time he awoke from his samadhi, he discovered that he was float-ing in midair one cubit from the ground. A moment later the stern dakini appeared yet again, warned him against the pride of achievement, and pointed to his meditation seat.

On the fourth occasion that he roused himself from his meditation, he found seven royal canopies floating above his head while seven damaru skull drums spontaneously filled the air with sound.

"No one can tell me now that I haven't reached my goal," he told his disciples. "Follow me to the island of Lankapuri off the shores of Sri Lanka. We will convert the heathen inhabitants to the Buddha's path."

With a retinue of three thousand disciples, Kanhapa set out for the city of Lankapuri. When they reached the straits dividing the mainland from the island, he decided to show off his prowess. As his wondering attendants watched from the shore, he began skipping across the surface of the water toward the island.

"Even my guru cannot do this," he said to himself. But no sooner had he spoken the fateful words than he sank like a stone beneath the surface of the waters. The waves soon deposited him, coughing and sputtering, on the edge of the sand. When he turned over on his back to spit the sand out of his mouth, he found himself staring up at his guru Jalandhara floating in the sky directly above him.

"Having a little trouble?" asked Jalandhara dryly.

Sheepishly, Kanhapa confessed his pride and its consequences. Jalandhara laughed uproariously, then took pity on the miscreant. "Go to Pataliputra, where the beneficent king, Dharmapala, reigns," he said. "There, look for a pupil of mine, a weaver by trade. If you do everything he tells you to do, you will be sure to attain the ultimate truth—which, may I say, you have yet to comprehend." At this he vanished.

Suddenly, the canopies and skull drums reappeared in the sky, and Kanhapa knew that his powers had been restored—he could once again walk on water and leave his footprints in solid stone. He and his retinue set out immediately for Pataliputra.

When they arrived, he left his three thousand disciples waiting outside the city. Confident that he could find the man he was looking for, he sauntered down the street of weavers. Using his penetrating gaze to snap the threads of each weaver's loom as he passed, he finally came to one man whose warp and woof spontaneously restrung themselves. At this, he knew he need look no farther. He bowed down before the weaver and walked about him in reverential circles. Then he begged the yogin to teach him the ultimate truth.

"Will you promise to do whatever I say?" asked the weaver sternly.

"I will," Kanhapa vowed.

The weaver then took him to the cremation ground, pointed to a fresh corpse, and said, "Eat a piece of that flesh."

Kanhapa knelt down, took out his knife, and began to cut into the body. "Not like that, you fool!" snapped the weaver. "Like this!" Instantly transforming himself into a wolf, the weaver leapt upon the corpse and began to tear at it ravenously. When he was done feeding, he changed himself back into human form. "You can only eat human flesh in animal form," he told his astonished pupil.

Next, the weaver squatted down and defecated. He then took one of the three pieces of excrement and gave it to his pupil. "Eat it!" he commanded.

"What if someone sees me?" Kanhapa protested. "No, I won't do it."

Whereupon the weaver ate one piece himself, gave the second to the celestial gods, and the third to the Naga serpents to take back to the netherworld.

They then returned to the city, where the weaver bought five pennies' worth of food and liquor. "Call your disciples, and we'll celebrate a communal *gana-cakra* feast," he ordered.

Kanhapa did as he was told. But he wondered how the weaver was planning to feed so many people when there wasn't even enough food for one.

When the communicants assembled, the weaver blessed the offerings and began to ladle out the food. As if by magic, endless quantities of rice, sweet meats, and every kind of delicacy appeared in the bowls. The feast lasted for seven days, and still there was no end in sight to the offerings.

"I can't swallow another bite," said Kanhapa in disgust. Throwing away his leftovers as an offering to hungry ghosts, he called his disciples to him, and they walked away.

But the weaver appeared before them and sang:

> Miserable children, what will you gain
> By running away?
> You are destroying yourselves
> By separating the emptiness of perfect insight
> From the active compassion of life.
> Floating canopies and skull drums are nothing

Compared to the realization
Of the true nature of reality.

But Kanhapa refused to listen. He traveled on and on, eventually arriving at the city of Bhadhokora, 450 miles east of his starting point. On the outskirts of the city he spied a lichee tree laden with ripe fruit. Beneath it sat a frail young girl, singing softly to herself.

Kanhapa greeted the girl and asked if he might pick some of the fruit.

She shook her head, no.

At this Kanhapa flew into a rage. "I won't be denied by the likes of you!" he shouted and plucked the fruit from the tree with his powerful gaze.

No sooner had each lichee fallen to the ground than the girl sent it directly back to its proper place with her equally powerful gaze, thus revealing her true dakini nature.

But Kanhapa was now too angry to comprehend the import of the experience. And instead of propitiating the dakini, he cursed her with a maledictory mantra so powerful that she began to writhe on the ground and bleed profusely from every orifice.

A crowd soon gathered around the stricken girl, and the situation quickly turned ugly. People began muttering to each other: "Buddhists are supposed to be kind. This yogin is bloodthirsty!"

Somewhere deep within Kanhapa the truth of these words sank home, and he returned to his senses. He removed the curse, but alas, it was too late. The girl had already uttered a countercurse upon him. He fell to the ground vomiting and bleeding violently. In deathly anguish he called his faithful dakini companion Bhande to him and begged her to go south to Sri Parvata Mountain and bring him back certain herbs that grew only on its slopes. These alone could cure him.

In much distress Bhande set out immediately, making a journey of six months in barely seven days. In the misty dawn on the steep mountainside she gathered the precious herbs and started on the return journey to Bengal. However, when she was only a day's journey from where she had left the suffering yogin, she chanced to meet an aged crone weeping brokenheartedly by the side of the road. Alas, Bhande failed to recognize the seductress who had cursed her master, and she stopped to see if she could aid the old woman in any way.

"Why are you weeping, mother?" asked the dakini.

"Isn't the death of Lord Kanhapa reason enough for tears?" sobbed the crone.

The news threw Bhande into a fit of deep despair. Angry that all her efforts had been for naught, she flung away the phial of healing herbs. Continuing on her way, she expected to see the smoke of the funeral pyre at every bend in the road. Instead, she found her master still alive but sinking fast. When he asked her feebly for the herbs, she broke into a storm of weeping and told him how she had been tricked.

Kanhapa prepared for death, knowing he had only seven days to instruct his disciples before he left his karmically matured body for the Paradise of the Dakinis. He taught them the sadhana that is now known as the "Beheaded Vajra Varahi."

After he had breathed his last, Bhande scoured the great above, the great below, and the earthly realms between for the mundane dakini who had taken Kanhapa's life.

Eventually, she discovered her quarry hiding in the branches of a *sambhila* tree. Whereupon Bhande grabbed the witch by her foot, flung her to the ground, and cursed her with a spell so terrible the dakini remained in a mordant state forever after.

ACINTA
The Avaricious Hermit

Mahamudra is imageless, objectless.
Within it, all phenomena become
Knowledge and pure awareness.
Within it, the ten thousand delusive thoughts
Are empty. All reality
Is Mahamudra.

꙰

Long ago in Dhanirupa there lived a man so poor that he was never certain of his next meal. But his fantasy life was very rich indeed. In fact, all his thoughts were centered on one unobtainable goal—to be rich. So tormented was he by this obsession that he couldn't bear to have others interfere with his dreaming. To this end he moved away from civilization and went to live alone with his fantasies in a little hut he built in the forest.

One day the yogin Kambala chanced upon his hermit's retreat. As they were sharing a frugal meal, Acinta poured his heart out to his visitor.

"Well, I see you've managed to escape from men and their chattering," said Kambala. "But tell me this: has your thinking improved since you've been here?"

"Unfortunately, no," the hermit confessed with a sigh. 'I'm still possessed by the desire for riches. But I do know this: if I could just get rid of this one thought my mind would be perfectly empty, for it's all I think about. Do you know of any way I could free myself of this foolishness?"

"As a matter of fact, I do," replied the yogin. "If you will promise to practice what I teach you, I'll give you instruction."

The hermit vowed to practice faithfully, and the guru gave him the Samvara initiation. Then he sang him this song of instruction:

Desire is like the child
Of a barren woman,
To free your mind of it
Visualize your body as the heavens
And each of your thoughts
As the stars in the sky.
In time, the god of wealth himself will appear.
And all your desires will be fulfilled.

In the solitude of the forest, the hermit meditated according to his guru's instruction. When the glittering radiance of the stars filled his mind, there was no room left for thoughts of gold. His obsession vanished, as did the stars themselves, into the boundless expanse of the heavens, and he became thought-free.

He sought out his guru to tell him that his mind had become empty, and Kambala sang him another song:

What is the nature of the sky?
Can you make something of it?
How can you desire it?
How can you think about it at all?

When the hermit realized the deep meaning within this verse, he achieved mahamudra-siddhi and became known as the guru Acintapa, "The Thought-Free Guru."

For three hundred years he selflessly taught his countless disciples how to realize the ultimate nature of being. And when the time came, they all accompanied him as he rose bodily into the Paradise of the Dakinis.

BHADRAPA
The Snob

Deluded vision can only be purified
By a clear vision of emptiness.
Deluded behavior can only be purified
By contemplating loving-kindness.
Meditation leads to the realization
That reality is all things made one,
And the goal is the pervasiveness of One Taste.

Long ago in the kingdom of Manidhara there lived a very proper, high-minded Brahmin who possessed untold riches. So conservative were his practices that not only had he never consumed pork or strong drink, he had never even spoken the words. No menstruating women were allowed anywhere in his environs lest he become defiled. And he would not think of risking his ritual purity by any manual labor or by coming into contact with filth or excrement.

Nevertheless, despite his wealth and position in society and the strictness of his observances, he constantly worried about how he appeared in the eyes of others. He was obsessed with maintaining his image untarnished.

One day, when his aristocratic friends had gone out to perform their ritual ablutions, he found himself alone in the house. When a disheveled yogin with matted hair appeared on his doorstep begging for food, he was forced to speak to the man himself.

In a desperate panic to get rid of the mendicant before anyone saw him, he ran toward the yogin waving his hands and shouting, "Out! Out! You are unclean. You defile my house!"

"What do you mean, unclean?" asked the yogin coolly.

"What do I mean by unclean?" said the Brahmin, observing his unwanted guest with a sneer. "I mean unwashed for years. Wearing filthy rags. Carrying a food bowl made of a human skull and stinking of rotting garbage. And you are quite obviously from a very low caste. Now please go before any of my friends see you."

The yogin stayed right where he was and gazed at the Brahmin unwaveringly. "That is not unclean," he said softly. "But I will tell you what is. Viciousness in speech, mind, and action—that is unclean. The subtle defilements of the mind—those are unclean. None of these can be removed by ritual bathing. Soap cannot cleanse the mind and heart. Only the pure bath of the guru's instruction can clean away such impurities."

Seeing that the Brahmin was listening to him intently, the yogin sang him this song:

> Neither priest nor king is the highest of beings,
> Only the Bodhisattvas.
> No amount of scrubbing
> Can cleanse body, speech, and mind,
> Only the precepts of the lineal guru
> Give matchless purity.
> No rich man's feast of milk, cheese, and curd
> Tastes the most sublime,
> Only desirelessness sets the best table.

The Brahmin was gaining confidence in the yogin by the minute and begged him for instruction.

"Give me food and I will teach you," said the yogin simply.

"Very well," agreed the Brahmin. But then he suddenly remembered how all this would look to his friends and added, "But not here. My friends have no faith. Let me come to your house and listen to you there."

"I live on the cremation ground," said the yogin, walking away. Then he stopped, as if deep in thought for a moment, and turned back to the Brahmin. "Bring some liquor and pork with you when you come."

"I can't do that," cried the Brahmin, horrified. "What if someone saw me?"

"If you want instruction, do as I say," said the yogin sternly.

"All right then," said the Brahmin, "but not before nightfall."

The yogin shrugged, then walked out on the dusty road and disappeared.

The Brahmin was in a quandary. How was he going to procure those two unmentionable items the yogin had demanded without causing a social scandal? Finally he hit upon a plan. He would disguise himself as a low-caste servant and shop undetected. Although the very idea disgusted him, he pulled it off successfully.

After dark he made his way stealthily to the cremation ground with the forbidden provisions. The guru welcomed him to his hovel, prepared the supper, and insisted the Brahmin share it with him. Afterward, the guru initiated his high-caste guest into the mandala of thanksgiving with a transfer of grace.

Then began a series of practices designed to break the Brahmin's pride of caste. As a symbolic demonstration of correct vision, the pupil was ordered to clean out his master's latrine, a hitherto forbidden task. And when he had completed this task, he was ordered to make plaster from the usual mixture of mud, excrement, and white lime and then replaster the yogin's hut. The guru explained that this was a symbolic demonstration of correct action. The white color of the lime represented the sameness of all things, which is the object of correct meditation.

When the Brahmin had done all these things to his master's satisfaction, the guru told him that all these acts symbolized the goal of practice. Whereupon the Brahmin suddenly understood that vision, meditation, and action were all one and the same, that all phenomena were both the same and equal. Then and there he forsook his caste and all its prejudices to become a yogin.

After six years of meditation, he achieved mahamudra-siddhi and became renowned far and wide as the yogin Bhadrapa, "The Auspicious Teacher." For the remainder of his life he worked selflessly for others. And when the time came for him to be assumed into the Paradise of the Dakinis, five hundred disciples were able to ascend with him.

KALAPA
The Handsome Madman

All these people live out their lives
In total delusion,
And yet such fools call me mad.
Ah, but I know that the cure for such delusion
Is the ambrosial nectar of the guru's precepts.

Kalapa's good karma was written all over him. The practice of patience and meditation in a previous life had endowed him with an athlete's body, exquisitely sculpted features, and dark, flashing eyes with soulful depths. He was so beautiful that the people of Rajapur would come to a dead stop in the street and gape after him as he passed by.

Unlike those people who trade on their beauty and manipulate people with it for their own selfish ends, Kalapa felt only pain and embarrassment from such attention. He came to believe that no one ever saw the flesh and blood human being beneath his outward appearance, that he was slowly being reduced to a mere art object. The more other people's attention removed him from the sphere of ordinary beings the more isolated and withdrawn he became.

Finally, he decided that the only course of action left to him was to renounce the world totally and retire to a cremation ground. And that's where he went, with the barest minimum of belongings, and built himself a tiny hut.

It wasn't long before he met a yogin who also lived on the cremation ground, and the two struck up a friendship.

The yogin listened to Kalapa's story with interest and sympathy. "I know a sadhana that might be just the thing to help you work through this predicament," he told the young man.

Kalapa was eager to learn, and his guru gave him the Samvara initiation. Then he was instructed to practice both the creative and fulfillment modes of meditation. The first would give him a vision of the phenomenal world free of all the constructs and prejudices of the mind. The second would permit him to realize the nature of all things as emptiness.

Soon he was able to practice both meditations together. This helped him understand that all appearances are but a function of the mind and can be reduced to a single thought, which is how the gods perceive their creation. When he had accomplished this, he also realized that he had lost the delusion of separateness, that there was no difference whatsoever between him and any-one else.

Free of all prejudices and emotional attachments, uninhibited action began to flow through him of its own accord. The doors of perception were thrown open, and he began to express his feelings and inclination without restraint or concern for social niceties.

The people of Rajapur, who had no notion of what it was like to experience reality directly, without fetters of the preconditioned mind, were dismayed. "Not another mad saint!" they cried.

Whereupon the divine madman sang:

> The roots of anxiety are embedded
> In the delusion that every one of us
> Is an island unto ourselves,
> Alone and separate, each from the other.
> If you would be free of this suffering,
> See the workings of your mind
> As but a single thought,
> A retinue of gods
> That vanish into the sound of "'A"
> As the rainbow vanishes into the heavens.

> Birth, life, and death have lost their hold
> Upon this madman.
> The action flowing freely through him
> Is pure pleasure;
> The realization of unimpeded clarity

Is pure pleasure;
Meditation upon the unobstructed sense fields
Is pure pleasure;
The goal attained without effort
Is pure pleasure.

So saying he levitated into the sky to the height of seven palm trees. Floating in the air, he demonstrated his control over all the elements by performing many wonders before the amazed populace.

Thereafter, he became famous near and far as the yogin Kalapa and in due course of time was assumed bodily into the Paradise of the Dakinis.

BHUSUKU (SANTIDEVA)
The Lazy Monk

In samsara, I was alienated from the Buddha
And lived only to savor various tastes.
Then realization united samsara and nirvana in bliss,
And I flamed like a jewel in the great ocean.

The younger son of a royal family came to the famed monastic academy of Sri Nalanda to be ordained in the mahasanghika order. But he had been much pampered as a child, and he found it not only difficult but unreasonable to give up his former ways. While his fellow monks studied, he lazed in bed. While his fellow monks spent hours in meditation, he strolled about the gardens of the monastery for the sake of his digestion. His other greatest pleasure was mealtime, where he savored every grain of his five measures of rice.

His lazy ways irritated his peers beyond belief, and they took to calling him Bhusuku, "The Shiftless One." They gossiped about him remorselessly behind his back, said equally rude things to his face, and dearly hoped he would soon meet his comeuppance.

It was the custom at Nalanda that scriptures were read around the clock, morning, noon, and night, in every one season and out the other. To maintain this tradition each monk took his turn sitting upon the temple throne under the monks' canopy reciting his memorized portion of the sutras. Every one took his turn, without exception, except of course Bhusuku. As he had managed to memorize nothing, he often missed his turn. The accumulated annoyance and enmity that arose from this was surprising in so holy an institution.

Finally, Bhusuku's scandalous behavior earned him a severe warning from the abbot. He was told that unless he mended his ways and took his turn on

the rota like everyone else, he would be expelled from the monastery. Quite a number of monks smirked behind their hands at this, evidently hoping for the worst possible outcome.

"But I've broken no vow," Bhusuku argued in his own defense. "I'm simply a bad scholar. Is that any reason for expelling me?"

The abbot was adamant. Tomorrow morning bright and early his turn came up. If he missed his recitation this time, he was out on his ear. The monks were delighted, and a good deal of petty gossip flew about concerning the imminent downfall of a certain good-for-nothing lazybones.

Despite his warning, however, the abbot was a very kindly man, and he had a soft spot for the miscreant. That night, after everyone had gone to bed to dream of the glorious comedy to come on the morrow, the abbot came to Bhusuku's cell to give him some advice.

"Well, my son," said the abbot, "you've gotten yourself into a pretty pickle. You've spent so much time pandering to your stomach and being a slugbed, you've not managed to learn so much as half a dozen lines of any one sutra. You will certainly fail tomorrow unless you follow my counsel."

Bhusuku prostrated himself at the abbot's feet and begged for his help. "Anything, sir. Just name it. I'll do it."

"Very well," said the abbot, adding sternly, "but it means you'll get no sleep tonight."

"Even that, sir," said the chastened monk.

"The only hope for you," said the abbot, "is to spend the night reciting the mantra of Manjusri, the Bodhisattva of Intellect. You must recite the *arapacana* mantra until cockcrow, and hope for the best." He then gave Bhusuku the secret precepts of Manjusri's sadhana, and the blessing of the mantra, and left the repentant one to his task.

Knowing his own weaknesses well, Bhusuku took the precaution of tying the collar of his robe to the ceiling by a stout cord lest he nod off during the night. And all night long he recited the mantra the abbot had taught him—over and over again until he was in a stupor of fatigue.

Just before the dawn, his cell was suddenly flooded with light. Bhusuku jerked awake and decided it must be sunup, and here he was, not one whit wiser than he'd been the night before. Just then a great voice boomed from the ceiling: "What do you think you're doing!"

Looking up, the exhausted monk saw an enormous figure floating in the air above his head. "I am invoking the aid of Lord Manjusri to help me recite a sutra this very day, and I have learned none. But who are you, and what do you want of me?"

"That's a foolish question," replied his unusual guest. "You've been invoking me half the night."

"Y-y-y-you are Manjusri himself!" stammered the startled monk.

"The very one. Now tell me what you want, and let me get on about my business."

Bhusuku would have flung himself to the floor, but he was still tied to the ceiling, so he pressed his palms together in the gesture of supplication and begged, "Please, great lord, grant me the power and realization of every quality of perfect insight."

"Done!" said Manjusri. "Recite your sutra when you are called." And he vanished as suddenly as he had come.

Word was abroad that Bhusuku was about to make a fool of himself this very day, and King Devapala and his entire court came for the show. The altar was piled high with the fragrant offerings of flowers all the visitors had brought with them.

The audience tittered and whispered to each other when Bhusuku arrived in the great hall. They were amused as he walked confidently down the aisle and mounted the temple throne—all waited eagerly for him to fall flat on his face. Instead, he called for the monks' canopy and seated himself in the lotus position. He gazed out at his audience with great calm and waited patiently for quiet. When it became clear that he at last had everyone's attention, he levitated into the air above the throne, and his body began to blaze with a great radiance that pulsed throughout the great hall.

Those who had come to laugh were stricken dumb with amazement. They looked at each other in wonder.

Bhusuku greeted the king and asked, "Shall I recite a traditional sutra, your majesty, or would you prefer something of my own composition?"

The king began to smile. "I am told that your eating habits are highly unusual," he said, "and your sleeping and strolling habits are subjects of great wonder to your fellow monks. It seems only fitting that you should maintain your standards of originality and recite a sutra of your very own."

Whereupon Bhusuku began to compose and recite the sublime and pro-found discourse that came to be called the Bodhicaryavatara, "The Pathway to Enlightenment." When he had completed the tenth and last chapter he rose into the sky to the height of seven palm trees, inspiring renewed faith in those who had assembled there that day.

"This is not Bhusuku, 'The Shiftless One,'" exclaimed the king. "He is surely a great sage." And he renamed the monk Santideva, "Divine Peace."

The people began to strew the places his feet had touched with flowers, and the pundits humbly requested a commentary on his discourse. Santideva obliged them, but when the monks entreated him to become their abbot, he refused.

That night, he left his robes, his begging bowl, and all his sacred artifacts upon the altar as an offering and departed secretly. Traveling from land to land, he finally arrived in Dhokiri, a town of some 250,000 households. There he fashioned himself a handsome sword out of a piece of wood and painted it with some gold paint. The following day he made his way to the court, prostrated himself before the king, and requested a position as swordsman with the palace guard. The king decided he was a likely looking fellow and hired him on the spot at the handsome stipend of ten *tolas* of gold a day.

Santideva served the king faithfully for twelve years. By day he lived as any other soldier. By night he practiced his sadhana, constantly attentive to the ultimate nature of reality. Every autumn, during the great festival of the Mother Goddess, Umadevi, he accompanied the guards to the temple just as though he, too, were a devotee.

No one was any the wiser about his true nature until one afternoon when everyone was in the armory polishing up their weapons and repairing their gear. One of the guards took a good look at Santideva's sword. It seemed to be made of wood! Thinking to do himself a service, the guard went off immediately to report his findings to the king and expose the imposter. Santideva was summoned to the throne room.

"Show me your sword," demanded the king.

"I would gladly do so, sire," said Santideva, "but it will do you great harm if I obey."

"Do as I say!" commanded the king. "Let me worry about the results."

As Santideva reached for the pommel, he pleaded, "At least cover one eye, sire."

Laughing among themselves, the king and all who were gathered there each covered one eye with a hand. Whereupon Santideva unsheathed the sword of awareness. As he pointed it heavenward, a light as intense as ten suns filled the throne room, blinding each unprotected eye. Everyone there, including the king, fell upon his knees before Santideva, entreating the yogin's forgiveness and mercy.

Santideva went to each person in the room, beginning with the lowliest servant, and, spitting on his forefinger, rubbed his healing saliva onto each injured eye, magically restoring the lost sight. The king begged him to remain as his palace priest, but Santideva declined and departed Dhokiri that very day.

He took up residence in a cave in the mountain fastness and lived there practicing his sadhana for some time. But he was always an object of curiosity hunters and woodsmen who lived roundabout, and they kept an eye on his doings.

One day, a royal huntsman came to court with rare game for the king's table and let it be known that, with his own eyes, he had seen Santideva hunting and killing deer and eating venison roasted upon a spit.

The king immediately set out for the mountains with a large entourage to investigate these serious charges. They came upon Santideva sitting on a deerskin meditating in front of what appeared to be a blank rock wall.

The king told the yogin all that he had heard, adding, "You who taught the king of Nalanda to swallow his pride and who restored the sight of myself and all my court, why with such power at your command are you harming beings?"

"I do not kill," said Santideva, "I heal." Whereupon he waved his hand in the air and the rock face opened behind him, revealing the entrance to his cave. Out sprang every imaginable sort of animal. As they went bounding off into the woods, they seemed to multiply before the amazed eyes of the king and his retinue until the creatures covered every hill and filled every valley. And then they vanished as though they had never been.

"All elements of experience are merely dreams and illusions," explained Santideva. "Understand that all things are but insubstantial figments of the imagination, projections of the mind. Enter the path of liberation." He then recited this verse:

> The deer I took for venison
> Never existed on this earth
> Yet will never cease to be.
> If there is no such thing as substance,
> Then there can be no hunter, no hunted.
> It is not I who am the lazy one here.

Whereupon Santideva converted the king of Dhokiri and set all his people upon the path of truth. He served them faithfully for one hundred years before ascending to the Paradise of the Dakinis.

KOTALIPA
The Peasant Guru

Both pleasure and pain are the mind's creations
Therefore heed the guru's instructions
And cultivate the mind for its own nature.
Even the wisest man may dig forever
On a mountain of rock
And never discover the natural state of bliss.

Awaken consciousness in the depths of your heart.
Drink deep of the six pleasure streams of the senses.
Do not seek to label, to name,
It only causes anxiety. In and out of meditation,
Relax in a tension-free state of natural ease.

Kotalipa was a good and honest man, a hard-working peasant whose life was an endless round of drudgery. Day in, day out, he toiled ceaselessly at plowing and planting a mountainside. The most meager of existences was his only reward.

One day, as he was digging out a terrace from the unforgiving stone, the master Santipa chanced to pass by, returning to his home in Magadha after converting the people of Sri Lanka.

"Who are you, and what are you doing there?" called Santipa.

"I am a peasant digging this mountain," answered Kotalipa, bowing low. "Why are you trying to grow crops on bare rock?" asked the master. "Once I had a beautiful farm with rich black soil," said Kotalipa sadly, "but it lay in the path of warring kings. They plundered and burned until there was nothing left for our

villagers to do but flee for our lives. Now all we have is this poor mountain, but at least we are safe."

"If you had a mantra for digging mountains and instruction to go with it, would you practice these precepts?" asked Santipa.

"Yes, holy one, indeed I would," replied Kotalipa, and he listened with care as Santipa spoke of the six perfections.

"While one may concentrate on physical suffering as the object of one's meditation," Santipa said, "without any understanding of the true nature of mind, it can become a death trap."

> Your body has been worn down by your hard life
> You have been following the karma
> Of six-fold perversity;
> Digging the earth as generosity;
> Nonviolence as moral conduct;
> Enduring pain as patience;
> Persistent effort as perseverance;
> Unflagging energy as concentration;
> Recognition of this path as perfect awareness.

> The karmic path is inherently hostile.
> You must abandon it and practice the karma
> Of six-fold perfection:
> Devotion to the guru as generosity;
> Guarding the mind as moral conduct;
> Constancy of mind's nature as patience;
> Meditation upon mind's nature as perseverance;
> Undistracted absorption as concentration;
> And perception of reality as perfect awareness.
> Practice these precepts and you will find release.

Kotalipa asked for more precise instruction.

"First, you must devote yourself totally to the guru," said Santipa. "Since the mind is the source of all pleasure and pain, you must come to recognize the purity of its nature. The mind is like a mountain, immutable, unchanging. Dig it with the spade of radiant knowledge. Just as each of your hands can perform different but complementary tasks simultaneously, learn to dig your mountain and meditate upon the true nature of mind at one and the same time.

> Without these precepts
> You may dig your life away on this mountain
> And never realize the pure pleasure
> Of the true nature of the mind.
> Therefore, hearken to the guru
> And cultivate the mountain of mind

For twelve years, with undistracted singleness of concentration, Kotalipa cultivated both the earth and mind, and he attained siddhi. After numerous selfless deeds for the welfare of all beings, he was assumed into the Paradise of the Dakinis.

INDRABHUTI
The Enlightened King

Without the spontaneous spark of grace
At exactly the right moment,
The yogin's awakening can never occur.
There is no difference between perfect bliss
And the Buddha. Cut through
The ties of attachment,
Experience blissfulness.

Oddiyana, the land of the dakinis, was divided into two kingdoms. King Indrabhuti ruled the 250,000 households of Sambhola, while King Jalendra reigned over the same number of households in Lankapuri. The sole difference between the two kingdoms was that King Indrabhuti's families worshiped the Buddha, and the other families worshiped Brahman. While both kings had managed to maintain a peaceful relation with each other, they realized that this harmony would be strengthened profoundly if a propitious marriage were to unite the two kingdoms.

Now it so happened that Indrabhuti had a seven-year-old sister who showed every promise of great beauty and intelligence. Knowing this, King Jalendra sent ambassadors with sumptuous gifts to the neighboring kingdom to beg Princess Laksminkara's hand in marriage for his only son. As religion was the sole obstacle, and it had not interfered with the peaceful relations between the two countries before, it was decided that this royal marriage was exactly what both kings had been seeking.

Not long after the official betrothal, the guru Lawapa, also known as Kambala, chanced to journey through Sambhola. Summoned to court, he

gave the king's wives and the little princess instruction. This so impressed Laksminkara that she began to practice her precepts with great earnestness.

A year later her betrothed came to meet his bride-to-be and to return with her to his own kingdom. All the people of Sambhola marveled at his magnificent entourage and the wondrous gifts of elephants, fine horses, gold, silver, and precious jewels he had brought with him from Lankapuri. The young people met briefly, but the prince was informed that she was much too young to leave the familiar surroundings of her home, and thus he returned empty-handed.

King Jalendra was surprised, but he accepted the explanations and did not press the wedding plans further until the princess was sixteen. Then he sent another magnificent escort bearing even more sumptuous gifts than before to bring the bride to her new home.

All this time, however, she had been practicing her sadhana and was loath to enter upon her new duties. In fact, the moment she arrived in the unenlightened kingdom of Lankapuri, a great revulsion for all the things of the world overcame her. She fled the palace late one night and went into the mountains to live in a cave.

In time the yogini-princess gained mahamudra-siddhi, the highest level of attainment. Whereupon she returned to the royal city and began teaching the Buddha's word to King Jalendra's latrine sweepers and the other outcastes of his kingdom. After years of selfless service she ascended into the paradise of the Dakinis.

Back in the days when the young bride had first arrived in her new home, her outrageous behavior scandalized the court and the country. King Jalendra immediately sent messengers to King Indrabhuti to enlist his aid in reasoning with his sister.

However, Indrabhuti's response was as surprising as Laksminkara's, for the news from Kankapuri had filled him with a sense of inadequacy that bordered on shame. "Here my baby sister has attained Buddhahood, and what have I been doing all this time?" he thought, "Living a life of complacency surrounded by ease and comfort. Laksminkara has fathomed the very mystery of existence, while all I've done is rule this country. I see clearly now that the burden of government must be a punishment inflicted upon me by my karma." He resolved to abdicate his throne and follow his sister's path.

After the coronation of his son, Indrabhuti retired from the world and went to live in a small palace where he practiced his sadhana for twelve years, secretly gaining mahamudra-siddhi.

One day his son came to visit him accompanied by those who had loved the old king dearly. As they were about to enter the palace, a loud voice rang out directly over their heads. Looking up, they were astonished to see Indrabhuti floating in the air above them seated upon a magnificent throne.

The visitors were all as happy as if they themselves had just reached the first level of the Bodhisattva's path, and they prostrated themselves before him. The king remained floating in the air for another seven days, instructing his son and his old friends on the doctrine of "inconceivable profundity and immensity."

On the eighth day, accompanied by seven hundred disciples, he was assumed bodily into the Paradise of the Dakinis.

JALANDHARA
The Chosen One

Allow blessings to rise within yourself
By gathering every thought, every concept
From the sensual, the aesthetic, and formless realms
Into the clarifying universe of body, speech, and mind:
The body of appearances
The speech of vibrations and pure form
The mind of pure consciousness.
Bind them in the three psychic channels:
The subjectiveness of the male lalana,
The objectiveness of the female rasana,
Which empty into the avadhuti, the all-embracing mind.

Jalandhara was a Brahmin who lived in Turkhara City. He was a man of great spirituality, and the more refined his consciousness became, the more he was disgusted by the life he saw around him. At last one day he walked away from his old life and all his possessions and went to live in a cremation ground. There he sat down beneath a sheltering tree and began to meditate. Soon he was absorbed into a blissful state in which he heard a dakini speaking to him from the skies.

"O noble son," said a voice of indescribable sweetness, "may you know the absolute truth."

Jalandhara was overcome with joy. Day after day he prayed to his dakini-guru until she actually manifested before his wondering eyes. She gave him the Hevajra initiation and empowerment, and then these instructions on fulfillment meditation:

"Gather all perceptions—inner and outer phenomena, the three realms, the

world of appearances in all its many forms. Place them in the subtle planes of body, speech, and mind.

"Next, empty all ideas, all mental constructs concerning body, speech, and mind into the subtle energies of the male and female psychic channels, the lalana and rasana. Then move beyond even this subtle duality into the central column of psychic energy, the pure awareness of the avadhuti. Eject all the outworn flotsam and jetsam of your former manner of perception through the gate of purity at the fontanel on the crown of your head.

"From that moment on, meditate solely upon the indivisibility of appearances and emptiness." And she recited these verses to Jalandhara:

> When all your thoughts about reality
> Have been gathered into body, speech, and mind,
> When the white and red streams of the lalana and rasana
> Have been poured into the purity of the avadhuti,
> When all that remains has erupted
> Through the heart of the thousand-petaled lotus,
> Then, in the space that is pure yoga,
> Know that emptiness is the most sublime pleasure.
> Try to sustain the inseparable union
> Of pure pleasure and pure emotion

Jalandhara meditated for seven years according to the instructions he had received from his dakini preceptress. At last, he gained mahamudra-siddhi. Many years later, after working selflessly for untold beings, he was assumed bodily into the Paradise of the Dakinis with three hundred disciples.

BHIKSANAPA
Siddha Two-Teeth

Like a tightrope walker,
The superior yogin with perfect balance
Steps out upon the high rope,
Its two strands of means and insight
Spun into the union of pure pleasure.
Following in the steps of the guru's precepts,
I attained the incomparable, inaccessible shrine
Of realization.

Once, long ago, a man of low caste who lived in Pataliputra met with good fortune. To his surprise an aged relation had died and left him a small legacy.

He had wanted so many things for so long that he went on a spree. Without a care for tomorrow, he went where the winds of desire blew him—here a tavern feast, there a new suit of clothes, and everywhere grasping friends to help him spend his fortune. Quicker than a wink, he was left with empty pockets, an empty stomach, and no friends.

Well, there was nothing for it now but to beg. And he went from town to town in search of a few scraps of food. One day, when he had had no luck and it seemed that his stomach would never know comfort again, he wandered off into the jungle to a remote and lonely spot where he could wallow in misery to his heart's content.

And there he sat, reviling himself and the world in an endless litany of sorrow until a dakini took pity on him. Appearing before him in all her splendor, she nearly startled the wits out of the poor man. But when gently, in the sweetest of voices, she asked what was troubling him, he took heart and told her all that had befallen him.

"I have the means to fulfill your desires," said the dakini.

"Then please, please teach me," he begged. "I have nowhere else to turn."

"What will you give me in return?" she asked.

He cast about him in futility for something to offer her, but he had nothing more than a few rags. Then he was suddenly struck by an odd idea. Whereupon he bit down with all his strength, completely fusing together an upper and lower tooth. Then he knocked out all his remaining teeth and presented them as an offering to the dakini.

This was a sign that he was capable of superior thought, for his action was an expression of the union of pleasure and emptiness—the dance of the dakini and guru. Then and there she gave Bhiksanapa initiation and instruction in the two-in-one union of skillful means and perfect insight.

After seven years of meditation, he saw the truth of this union. The inexhaustible virtue and power of the Buddhas arose in his mindstream, and he attained his goal. He became known as Siddha Two-Teeth and continued to roam from village to town begging his food, but now he did it for the sake of those ready for instruction. After many years he was assumed into the Paradise of the Dakinis.

GHANTAPA
The Celibate Monk

To evoke blessings in oneself
Bind tight the three psychic channels
Of the lalana, rasana, and the avadhuti.
To gain realization in oneself
Attend to three things—
The guidance of the guru,
The nature of the mind,
The purity of phenomena.

Ghantapa was the son of the king of Nalanda, but he renounced the throne and became a famed and learned monk at the monastic academy. Years later, dissatisfied, seeking, he renounced the monastic life and became a wandering yogin. In his travels he met the guru Darikapa and was initiated into the Samvara mandala.

Following the instructions of his guru, Ghantapa traveled to Pataliputra, where King Devapala ruled over 3,100,000 house holds. The monk took up residence under a spreading tree just where the edge of the royal city met the jungle. There he begged alms and practiced his sadhana.

King Devapala was himself a pious and devout man. For many years he had welcomed innumerable monks and yogins within the borders of his kingdom, but despite his charitable works, he still felt that he had not accumulated enough merit for his next rebirths. This troubled his mind to such an extent that his wife asked him if he was ailing; should she call the court physician?

He confided his spiritual difficulties to her and asked her advice. His wife thought for a moment, then clapped her hands in delight. "It is the workings of

karma that you have told me this today, for I have just learned that a great saint and strict observer of moral conduct has arrived in our kingdom. He has just placed his mat under a tree on the outskirts of town."

"But, my dear," objected the king, "I have already patronized any number of holy men, and my mind is still troubled."

"This one is different," insisted the queen. "I feel it in my bones. The important thing now is to get him to take up residence in the palace. Surely his daily guidance will help you achieve the highest state. Since he is a man who possesses nothing but his robes and a few necessities and must beg his daily food, let us offer him a magnificent feast in his honor." Carried away by this idea, she began to compose the menu—"eighty-four main dishes of the rarest curries; fourteen kinds of the most delectable sweetmeats; wine of the finest grapes and the five kinds of beverage. It will be a feast fit for the gods themselves. He surely cannot refuse our hospitality."

The king was the most generous of men, and this idea appealed to him greatly. The following morning he sent his servants to invite Ghantapa to the palace. But to everyone's surprise, the master refused the invitation, and the emissaries returned alone.

The next day the king went in person to the master's tree, accompanied by a great retinue. Prostrating himself before Ghantapa, the king made the most eloquent plea for him to come to the palace.

"I gave you my answer yesterday," said Ghantapa. "Why did you bother to come?"

"To offer you my charity and to show you how much faith I place in your holy presence," replied the king.

"Your kingdom is filled with vice," said Ghantapa sharply. "I will not come."

The king was stung by these words—had he not lived the most exemplary of lives? Nevertheless, he persisted. "I beg your indulgence. Please come to the palace and live with us for one year."

Again Ghantapa refused. The king bargained for a visit of six months, then three months, then two weeks, and finally one hour.

"Never, never, never," said Ghantapa adamantly. "Every movement you make, every action you take, every thought you think, every word you say is sin filled. Keep your feasts and your earthly delights. I want none of them."

Every day thereafter for forty days the king returned to Ghantapa's tree to repeat his invitation to the palace. And every day for forty days Ghantapa refused.

Finally, their pride wounded to the quick, the king and queen grew to hate Ghantapa. And where they once would hear only good spoken of him, now they wished to hear only evil tales.

Hate burning in his heart, the king had this decree broadcast to the four corners of his kingdom: "Whoever can prove that this boastful monk's virtue and chastity are merely sham will gain half my kingdom and one hundred weight in pure gold."

This bit of royal pique chanced to fall upon the ears of one Darima, a fabled courtesan who resided in Pataliputra. Now Darima was the most cunning whore who ever lived, and when she heard the proclamation she saw her chance for great wealth and power.

In her finest clothes, accompanied by a retinue of servants, she went to the palace and requested an audience with the king.

"Your majesty," she said, "your deepest desire is soon to be fulfilled. I have not the slightest doubt of my ability to cause the downfall of this troublesome monk."

"Then do your utmost," replied the king, who was himself much taken with her beauty and intelligence.

But Darima was even wilier than the king had supposed. It was not herself she planned to offer to the monk. Oh, no. She had another surprise up her silken sleeve. Darima had a twelve-year-old daughter, a virgin whose radiantly beautiful face, seductive gait, sweet intelligent speech, voluptuous hips, and shapely breasts caused the sun to halt in its path whenever it caught sight of her. It was her daughter's amazing combination of sensual beauty and pristine purity that Darima counted upon to ensnare the monk.

So saying, Darima went to visit Ghantapa every morning at dawn for ten days. Each day she prostrated herself before him and walked round about him in reverential circles. For nine days she said nothing, offered him nothing but her devotion. On the tenth day she begged, "Please allow me to be your patron during the summer monsoon retreat."

Ghantapa refused her as he had refused the king. But Darima returned again and again each sunup for a month as the clouds began to gather in the sky. She pleaded to be allowed to serve him—all she offered was the hospitality of her estate. Finally, seeing no harm, Ghantapa agreed.

Returning to her establishment, Darima was beside herself with glee. She decided to celebrate her coming success and invited all her friends and patrons to a great feast. That night as she made merry, she constantly sang a little song to herself under her breath:

> With sex as her unfailing weapon
> A woman's deceits fulfill her desires.
> Guile such as mine can seduce the world,
> A monk for all his holiness is only a man!

When the rains came, Ghantapa retreated to a little hut Darima had had constructed for him at the far edge of her property where the jungle bordered the road. Warily, the monk insisted that only male servants bring his food. Darima said she would humbly agree to his every wish. And for the first two weeks she sent waiters with simple meals of rice and cool spring water.

On the fifteenth day she had a luscious feast prepared. And calling her daughter to her rooms, she dressed her in all the silks and jewels of a princess. Then she sent her to wait upon the master with a train of fifty servants bearing trays of delicacies. The men were to carry the dishes to the edge of the clearing where the master's shelter stood and then return, leaving the heavenly scented food and the exquisite virgin before him.

"Who are you?" Ghantapa asked suspiciously when he caught sight of this vision.

"I am here to serve you today," said the beautiful girl, her voice and manner sweetly seductive. "The waiters had more pressing duties."

Offering him this dainty and that, she managed to linger until the afternoon storm clouds arose.

"You must leave now!" Ghantapa ordered sternly.

"Oh, please, holy sir," she said, peering worriedly at the sky. "I see clouds of five different colors. There will surely be a downpour any moment. And this is the only shelter for miles."

As if on cue, thunder crashed in the heavens and the rain swept down in torrents. Grudgingly, the monk agreed to share his hut if she kept her distance.

Not until sunset did the storm let up, during which time she plied the unsuspecting monk with shy smiles and tender blushes.

But this had no effect upon him. When the rain stopped he ordered her to return home.

"Good, sir," she said trembling, her eyes wide with fear, "surely you will not send me out after dark on the road alone. There are robbers and footpads who will surely slit my throat for the jewels I wear."

Knowing her fears were not unfounded, Ghantapa gave her permission to sleep outside the hut. But during the night she became frightened by the unfamiliar surroundings. In a sweet, plaintive voice she begged for his protection. With a sigh of resignation Ghantapa allowed her to come inside once again.

The hut was very tiny. The sleepers were very restless. Inevitably, their bodies touched. Then their limbs intertwined. Before long, they had passed through the four levels of joy and traversed the path of liberation to its ultimate fulfillment.

In six previous lives this very same girl had been the monk's downfall. Six times she had caused him to break his vow. But that was before his mind had become purified, before he had lost the yes and no, the subjective–objective duality of clouded eyes. But in this life such defilements had long since dissolved into the infinite expanse of emptiness, and he had gained the true path.

In the morning he asked the girl to remain with him, and she agreed. They became yogin and consort. And because of her service to him for six lives, the defilements of Ghantapa's consort's mind were also purified.

One year later their child was born.

During this time the king grew impatient for his triumph over the saintly monk. And he sent message after message to Darima demanding to know whether she had made any progress. But the canny courtesan knew how to bide her time. For three years her replies to the king were an artful combination of evasiveness and tantalizing promises of success.

Her spies kept her informed of all that went on in the little hut with its three occupants. Finally, Darima felt the time had come to go to the king and tell him that sweet revenge was now surely his.

The king was overjoyed, his outraged sense of morality would soon be assuaged and that holier-than-thou monk would get his comeuppance. "Send word to your daughter and the monk," said the king, "that I will come to visit them in three days' time."

When they heard the news, the girl was very fearful of the people's scorn and abuse, and she worried about the safety of her child. Ghantapa asked her whether she wanted to stay and face them down, or leave Pataliputra and take shelter in another land. She begged him to flee with her, and he agreed.

On the appointed day the king gathered all the people of his realm to witness the monk's degradation. Mounting his gorgeously caparisoned elephant, he rode at the head of the jeering, gleeful parade of the faithful toward the yogin's hut.

Meanwhile, Ghantapa and his consort made preparations to leave. The monk hid the child inside his robe, took a jug of liquor under his arm, and set out with his wife, who was carrying their few household possessions.

Alas, they failed to hear the oncoming mob, and as they rounded a bend in the road, they came face to face with the king and the multitude.

Tasting the sweetness of revenge, the king looked down on the fleeing pair from the grand height of his royal elephant. "What are you carrying, and what is that hidden under your robe?" he demanded in a voice like thunder. "Who is this girl, and why is she in your company?"

Ghantapa halted in the middle of the road. He looked the king straight in the eye and, in a voice twice as loud, replied, "I'm carrying a jug of liquor."

The crowd gasped.

Opening his robe, he held up the child. "I have my son under my robe."

The crowd began to turn ugly.

"And this is my consort," he said, putting his arm around the girl.

At this the crowd began to shout imprecations at the little family and call for every manner of punishment. But the king held up his hand for silence.

"So," said the king, savoring every moment, "the monk who refused to come to my palace because I was a sinful man has a whore's daughter as a lover with whom he has produced a bastard child, and to top it all off—he drinks liquor!"

"I am without fault," replied Ghantapa calmly. "Why do you insult me?" Again, the king repeated his accusation. And again the crowd began to make catcalls. Finally, Ghantapa hurled both his son and the jug of liquor onto the ground. This so frightened the earth goddess that she trembled with fear. The ground gaped open and a geyser of water spurted forth.

The child was instantly transformed into a thunderbolt and the jug of liquor into a bell. Whereupon the yogin, bearing thunderbolt and bell, levitated with his consort into the sky, where they became the deities Samvara and Vajra Varahi joined in father-mother union. They hovered over the heads of the king and the multitude as the waters rose higher and higher.

"We take refuge in the master!" screamed the drowning people. But Ghantapa remained adamant in his samadhi of immutable wrath.

As death seemed imminent, and all were on the point of drowning, the

Bodhisattva of Compassion suddenly appeared. Avalokitesvara placed his holy foot over the source of the flood, and the waters immediately flowed backward into the ground.

Everyone was saved. Prostrating themselves in the mud—even the king—they all begged Ghantapa for forgiveness. As if by magic, a stone image of the Bodhisattva appeared where his foot had trod. It remains there to this very day, and a spring of the purest water gushes forth to a height of six feet right next to the statue's foot.

Still hovering above the penitent assemblage, Ghantapa said: "Moral concepts practiced without understanding can be the greatest of obstacles to fulfilling the Bodhisattva's vow of uncompromising compassion. Do not cultivate virtue and renounce vice. Rather, learn to accept all things as they arise. Penetrate the essence of each experience until you have achieved the one taste." And then he sang them this song:

> While medicine heals and poison kills,
> Their ultimate essence is the same.
> Both positive and negative qualities
> Are aids on the path—
> The sage rejects nothing.
> Yet the unrealized fool
> Five times poisoned
> Is lost forever in samsara.

At this the king and all his people were illuminated. Like clouds before a brisk wind, their self-righteousness and petty prejudice vanished, and faith was born in the lotus center of each heart.

Ghantapa came to be known as "The Bearer of the Bell," and his fame rang out to all the corners of the earth. Possessing the glorious power and virtue of a Buddha, the yogin ascended into the Paradise of the Dakinis with his consort.

CAMPAKA
The Flower King

Like the clear light of means and insight united
The guru's constant flow becomes all embracing.
Sahaja, a wish-fulfilling tree,
Spontaneously emerges from the ground of being;
Its fruit, the trikaya, is radiant perfection.

The kingdom of Campa was named after the lushly perfumed flowers that grew so abundantly within its borders. Even the king himself took his name from the beautiful magnolia-like blossoms. In Campaka's realm there were flowers everywhere, and riches and pleasures of all sorts bloomed profusely for all his fortunate subjects.

The young king reveled in the elegance and refinement of his court, enjoying his power and good fortune to the fullest. Life was such an endless succession of delights that he gave little thought to the future.

One day a yogin came to the palace begging for alms. The king received him in his little summer house, set like a jewel among radiantly blossoming campaka bushes. Sweet-smelling blossoms cushioned the throne and cascaded down into a carpet of velvety petals. Amid this riot of fragrance, the king washed the yogin's feet and gave him soft cushions to recline upon. Then he ordered a sumptuous repast for his guest and sat back to listen to the yogin's discourse.

So impressed was Campaka with what he heard that he asked the yogin to remain with him and become his priest. The yogin agreed.

"Tell me," said Campaka, as he was giving the yogin a tour of his palace and gardens, "you have traveled through many different countries—have you ever seen such flowers as these, or met a king like myself?"

"Nowhere have there been such flowers—their beauty and fragrance is beyond compare," replied his guest.

The young king beamed with pride.

"However," the yogin continued, "because of the heedless manner in which you live, the odor of your own body is far from agreeable. And, yes, your kingdom far surpasses many others, but what does it matter when even you must exit this world empty-handed?"

The king was stunned. For the first time in his life, he began to think beyond the pleasures of the day, and to examine the deeper questions of life, death, and rebirth.

Several days later he went back to his guru, told him what he learned from this introspection, and begged for further instruction that would destroy all attachment to his body. The yogin taught his young pupil about karma—the laws of cause and effect that govern all human activity—in order to discipline his mind in the ways of compassionate awareness and virtuous conduct. Then he initiated him into the path of creative and fulfillment yoga.

The king set to work on his meditative practices with all the will in the world. But he was constantly assailed by doubts as to whether or not he was meditating properly. And again and again, no sooner had he centered his mind than the heady scent of the campaka flowers would distract him.

In despair he returned to the yogin for assistance. And his guru devised a way for him to use these very distractions as stepping stones on the path:

> Know the nature of appearances as emptiness—
> That is the flower that is the guru's instruction
> Wherein the mind must settle like the hungry bee
> To gather the pollen that becomes endless ambrosia.
> There are no distinctions
> Between the flower, the bee, or the pollen,
> They are one in their essential nature.
> And the honey! The honey is pure pleasure.
> Thus taught Mahavajradhara, the Sixth Buddha himself.
> Meditate without doubt, without fear.

Campaka meditated upon the flower of pure reality for twelve years. In time he realized the truth of his guru's words about the emptiness of appearances. Instinctively, he grasped that the reality of his own mind was totally inseparable from the peak experience that he sought and thus attained his goal. Known as the Guru Campakapada, he instructed his court and consorts in the dharma for many years before he was assumed bodily into the Paradise of the Dakinis.

KUMBHARIPA
The Potter

Upon the whirling wheel of habitual action
The music and dance of existence takes form.
But the flames of knowledge and pure awareness
Will burn away all delusion.

Kumbharipa was a potter in the town of Jomanasri. Day in and day out his life was an endless round of digging clay, kneading clay, shaping it upon his wheel, and firing his pots. One evening, when he thought he could not bear to set the wheel spinning one more time, a yogin chanced to pass by begging his food.

Kumbharipa welcomed him in and shared his humble meal. And then he opened his heart to his visitor.

"Guruji," he cried, "I can't stand another minute at this potter's wheel. My life is nothing but endless toil and endless tedium."

The yogin gazed for a time at the potter's wheel, and then he gave it a spin. "Don't you understand that all beings on the wheel of rebirth never find a moment of true happiness? From time before time there has only been suffering. Don't get trapped in your own little misery. All human joys and pleasures are but fleeting shadows."

These words resonated in the potter's depths, and he begged the yogin to teach him a sadhana. Whereupon the yogin gave him initiation and instructed him in creative and fulfillment meditation with this verse:

> From the soil of unknowing and ignorance
> Comes the clay of passion and thought
> To be turned on the wheel of greed and grasping.

179

Fashion six pots from the six realms
Of samsaric ignorance and delusion,
Then fire the pots in the flame of pure awareness.

The potter understood the guidance of his guru, and he meditated for only six months—one month for each realm of samsaric illusion—before all the defilements of his mind were erased and he attained his goal.

As he sat in meditation, the potter's wheel spun all by itself, and pots sprang from it as joy sprang from the potter's heart. When the townspeople learned that he had gained the power of the Buddhas, they sat at his feet ready for instruction. In time, after many years of service, he was assumed into the Paradise of the Dakinis.

GODHURIPA
The Bird Catcher

Perceiving all inner and outer phenomena as mind,
Realizing the nature of mind as light,
Waking, sleeping, dreaming, meditating
In the dharmakaya,
I realized fully awakened Buddhahood.

Godhuripa came from Disunagar and was, by trade, a bird catcher. One day he was in the jungle netting small songbirds to sell in the marketplace when he chanced to meet a yogin on his way into town to beg food.

When the yogin saw him with his nets filled with tiny helpless creatures, he asked Godhuripa why he was doing such a cruel thing.

"I know it's wrong," said Godhuripa. "I suppose the many evils of my past lives have forced me into this violent trade in order to live. I'm ashamed of this miserable existence, but it's all I know how to do."

"My dear man," said the yogin, "don't you know that if you make your bad karma even worse by plying this trade, your future lives will be more miserable still?"

Godhuripa sat down beneath a tree and began to weep bitterly. At last, he looked up at the yogin, his eyes red and swollen, and begged for help.

"If you are willing to practice a sadhana," said the yogin, "you would come to find constant happiness in your net instead of constant sorrow."

"If a holy man such as yourself is willing to take pity on a sinner like me, how can I refuse?" said Godhuripa humbly.

Whereupon he released all the little songbirds from his nets and the yogin granted him initiation through a transfer of grace. Then the guru instructed

Godhuripa in the meditation that concentrates all attention on one dominant image.

"Visualize all the sounds in the world as your memory of birdsong, until sound and birdsong become one," said the yogin.

> Let your mind melt into the essence
> Of the nightingale's sweet song.
> When all sound becomes this one sound,
> Pierce the heart of the nightingale's cry
> And find the sound of silence,
> Wherein sound and the hearer of sound
> Are seen as all-embracing space.

Godhuripa meditated in this fashion until all sound had become one sound, inseparable from emptiness. After nine years all the defilements of his perception had vanished into perfect silence, and he gained mahamudra-siddhi.

He remained in the world for another one hundred years working for all sentient beings, and then, with three hundred disciples, he arose bodily into the Paradise of the Dakinis.

KAPALAPA
The Skull Bearer

The oneness of the Vajradhara—
The nonduality of all phenomena—
The secrets of the six ornaments and skull,
The delusory ego itself:
None of these can be found by seeking.

An epidemic of fever raged in the city of Rajapuri. The beloved wife of a low-caste laborer died in great torment and distress in the arms of her grief-stricken husband. Although his five small sons were also ill with the fever, the widower was forced to leave them to carry his wife's body to the cremation ground.

As he sat beside the corpse, weeping brokenheartedly, even more tragic news was brought to him. All five of his children had also died of the treacherous disease. On the saddest journey of his life, he brought their five little bodies to lay beside their mother's. There were no more tears in him.

Overwhelmed with loss, he just sat there, silently rocking back and forth beside what had once been his loving family.

The guru Krsnacarya appeared and sat down by him to offer comfort.

"Yogiji," said the poor man, his voice leaden, "you see before you the end of all my happiness. There is nothing left for me in life. All I can think to do is remain here next to my family until I die too."

"All beings of the three realms live under a cloud of death," said the yogin. "This suffering has not come to you alone. But since you feel you can no longer be of use to yourself or others, why not practice a sadhana?"

The bereaved laborer begged for his teachings, and the yogin initiated him

into the mandala of Hevajra. Then he gave him instruction in the creative and fulfillment stages of meditation.

From the bones of his little sons, the yogin carved for him the ornaments of the five Dhyani Buddhas—the crown, earrings, necklace, bracelets, and belt, and the trident of the dakini. Next, he attached the sacred thread. Lastly, Krsnacarya decapitated the wife's corpse, and from her head he fashioned a skull bowl.

"Visualize this skull as the form of creative meditation," he said, handing it to his disciple. "See the emptiness it contains as fulfillment meditation."

Kapalapa meditated in this fashion for nine years until he united both forms of meditation and achieved his goal. Then he sang of his realization to his own disciples:

> I am the yogin of the skull.
> I have come to see this skull
> As the very nature of all things.
> My activity is now without impediment.

After this revelation, he worked selflessly for others for five hundred years. When the time came, he ascended bodily into the Paradise of the Dakinis with six hundred disciples.

CARBARIPA (CARPATI)
The Siddha Who Turned People to Stone

The supreme vow of all the Buddhas
Is simply self-realization.
Whoever realizes the purity of his own mind
Sees through the Buddha's eyes.

In Magadha there once lived a wealthy herdsman who owned a thousand water buffalo and countless goats, sheep, and horses. It happened in the fullness of time that his aging father died and, according to custom, it was incumbent upon the herdsman to give a great funeral feast to which the entire district would be invited.

Early one morning during the ceremonial gathering, the family and all the guests went down to Mother Ganga to bathe in her purifying waters, leaving the herdsman's young wife in charge of the household and the day's preparations.

As she went about her tasks with her baby son on her hip, the guru Carbaripa suddenly materialized before her and asked for food. She prostrated herself before the holy man and burst into tears.

"Oh, sir, it would be my great privilege to serve you. But my husband and mother-in-law are very strict. They beat me when I do not carry out their instructions exactly. I was not given permission to feed anyone but themselves and our guests, and I am afraid to disobey."

"There, there," said the yogin, wiping away her tears. "Look up on that hill," he said, pointing into the distance. "Do you see my hut up there?"

The young woman shaded her eyes and gazed up at the hill. "Why, yes, I do believe I see something just there by the trees," she said.

"Good," said the guru. "If your husband or mother-in-law gives you the least bit of trouble about your feeding me my breakfast, you bring your baby and come right up there. I'll protect you."

The young wife was heartened by his reassurances and busied herself in the kitchen, offering a sumptuous meal to her visitor. He spoke with her at length, and she listened with increasing interest to his words.

No sooner had he departed than her mother-in-law returned with all the hungry guests from their morning bath. When the older woman saw how much food was missing, she raised such a terrible storm, scolding and screaming at the poor young wife, that even the baby began to howl. The terrified young woman fled from the house with her precious infant and didn't stop for a moment until she came to Carbaripa's hermitage.

The yogin came out to meet her with a smile of welcome. "How nice to see you again," he said, taking the squalling infant from the exhausted mother.

The child immediately began to smile and coo, and he returned it to its mother's arms, where it fell asleep in moments. Then he dipped his hand in a bowl of consecrated water and sprinkled it over his visitors. At the first touch of the waterdrops, both mother and child were transformed into stone images of the Buddha—no longer in need of either food or shelter.

In the meantime, the herdsman returned to his home and asked after his wife. Still fuming, his mother launched into yet another litany of his wife's wrongdoing, adding, "The stupid, shiftless good-for-nothing has run off, I'll have you know. And she's taken your son with her!"

The distressed husband sent out search parties in every direction. Morning, noon, and night they scoured the countryside to no avail. At dawn the grieving husband decided to climb to the top of the hill to get a better view, and who should he meet but the yogin.

"Welcome," said Carbaripa and sprinkled him with the consecrated water. He, too, was transformed into a stone image of the Buddha, and the yogin placed the three images—husband, wife, and child—upon a small stone pedestal.

Later in the day the other searchers began to make their way to the top of the hill, some alone, some in small groups. Carbaripa welcomed them all and sprinkled them all. By nightfall nearly three hundred people had come to the hermitage, and all had become Buddhas of stone—frozen in perfect meditation.

In this fashion the herdsman's young son gained the eight great siddhis: From his testicles came *khecari-siddhi;* from his penis came the nectar that transmutes base metal into gold; from his anus came the ambrosia of deathlessness; from his eyes came the power of flight; and on and on.

The fame of the miraculous child spread near and far—even the king of Campa came to pay his respects. He was so impressed with what he found that he had a temple erected for the child and his parents, and he had an even larger one built to house the remaining stone images.

Over the years these hilltop temples took on a great aura of holiness and power. Many people made pilgrimages there to practice their sadhana.

There is a legend that has grown up over the years that whenever any of the yogins meditating in this place falter in their practice or become bedeviled by intractable thoughts, the stone images regain their human form and beat them until their minds clear.

KANTALIPA
The Rag Picker

With the true guru of knowledge as my needle
And compassion as my thread,
I stitch the three realms together
Into the yogin's radiant garment.

Kantali was an outcaste, born to the miserable trade of piecing and stitching rags together into reusable cloth, like his father and grandfather before him. Not for one moment had he known either pleasure or a full belly. All life had ever meant to him was a continual round of work and misery.

One day, plying his trade, he accidentally jabbed his finger with his needle, and it bled profusely all over the cloth he had been working on for hours. Driven beyond all endurance, he ran out of his hovel and off to a secluded place in the forest. There he rolled upon the ground tearing at his hair and howling like a wounded animal.

Taking pity upon him, the dakini Vetali, the embodiment of the emptiness of the elements, appeared before him in the form of a kindly old woman and asked the cause of his despair.

Kantali told her of his life from the depths of his aching soul.

"What your story tells me," said the dakini, "is that you have suffered some great pain in your past life. And I fear that in your next life and the next and the next that pain will hound you like your shadow hugs your heels. There is nothing but pain to be found on the Wheel of Rebirth."

Kantali moaned and writhed on the ground. "Please, please," he begged, "can you show me how to avoid this terrible fate?"

"I could teach you a sadhana," she suggested, "but do you think you are capable of following it?"

"If you will only show me the way," he replied fervently, "there is nothing that could prevent me from following it."

Then and there the dakini gave him the Hevajra initiation and empowerment. She instructed him on the four boundless states of mind and taught him the yoga of identification with the guru as well as fulfillment yoga.

The rag stitcher returned home and did his best to follow her guidance. But whenever he tried to meditate, his wandering thoughts kept coming back to his work again and again.

Once more the dakini appeared to him and counseled, "Use these very thoughts to guide you on the true path." And she sang him this song:

> Envision the rags you pick and stitch as empty space.
> See your needle as mindfulness and knowledge.
> Thread this needle with compassion
> And stitch new clothing
> For all the sentient beings of the three realms.

Kantali returned to his work in great peace and used this meditational technique to realize the emptiness of all the elements of experience. As he did so, a great fount of compassion welled up within him. When he understood that compassion and emptiness were one, he gained mahamudra-siddhi. Working selflessly for others for many years, in time he ascended to the Paradise of the Dakinis.

JAYANANDA
The Crow Master

My kingdom is samadhi,
The realm of pure awareness and knowledge.
There, I abide in innate purity, free from duality,
Free from preconception and discursive thought.
My realization has assured my freedom.

In Bengal, long ago, there lived a Brahmin priest who had been converted to the practices of tantric Buddhism. Maintaining his outer life as it was, he secretly practiced the Tantric mysteries. Among his offering were tormas, little cakes specially prepared and consecrated to represent the body of the deity. After tasting the tormas during the course of a ceremony, he followed the custom of throwing the remainder upon the ground for the benefit of the dogs, and birds, and hungry ghosts. A large flock of crows, who are very intelligent beings, soon became aware of this practice and waited each day at the appointed time for their sacramental feast.

A jealous neighbor, another Brahmin priest whose ways were very strict and conservative, noticed this daily congregation of crows outside Jayananda's house and took to spying upon him. He speedily discovered his neighbor's apostasy and wasted no time in reporting his findings to the king, a staunch foe of Buddhism.

The king ordered Jayananda brought to him in chains.

"There is no sin or waste in making offerings to the gods," said the prisoner in reply to the king's accusations, "release me from these bonds!" But the king was adamant and ordered Jayananda incarcerated in the depths of the palace prison.

Later that day, as the hour for the ritual feast grew near, the faithful congregation of crows gathered outside the Brahmin's house. In vain they waited for the tasty cakes. Growing angry and restless, they dispatched scouts to spy out the whereabouts of their benefactor. Imagine their outrage when they learned that he was chained to the wall of a dungeon.

Like thunderclouds gathering in the distance, the vast ebony flock filled the sky as they converged on the palace of the king. Flying through every open door and window, the crows descended upon the throne room, diving at people's heads and pecking at their eyes and hands. Bleeding people ran screaming from the attack, but there was no place to hide.

Finally, a man who understood the language of the birds hurried to the king, who was hiding under his throne, and told him that the crows were demanding the release of a certain Brahmin who was their father and mother.

The besieged king immediately sent for Jayananda. The moment the Brahmin appeared, the birds settled down on every available perch. Like an ominous black fog, they awaited the outcome.

The king prostrated himself before the Brahmin and begged his forgiveness. Then he pleaded with Jayananda to send the crows out of the palace and back into the sky where they belonged, vowing that he would personally see to it that they never went hungry again.

The Brahmin spoke gently to his feathered family, and as one bird they took wing and mounted into the heavens. The king was filled with great faith at this sight, and he and all his court took refuge in the Buddha.

Every day thereafter, at the king's command, 20 cartloads of rice were scattered to the crows and distributed to the poor and needy.

The guru remained for many years in Bengal, working for the benefit of all creatures. And quite often he would sing this song:

> Listen, all of you who need to know,
> Listen to Jaya's words of victory:
> By the grace of the guru, perfect realization
> Became mine. My treasury is filled with
> Innate, spontaneously arising awareness.
> Now I am the minister of pure pleasure
> Who no longer attends the court of samsara.

My king is the naturally radiant nature of being
Who defeats the hostile powers of duality,
Detached from all worldly pleasure.

After seven hundred years of selfless service, Jayananda was assumed into the Paradise of the Dakinis.

DHILIPA
The Epicure

When I realized my Buddha nature
The Buddha became the nature of reality.
Empowered by the innate absolute,
I am permeated by the unborn Vajradhara.

Dhilipa was a merchant, whose business was pressing oil from sesame seeds. So lucrative was this trade that Dhilipa soon became as wealthy as Kubera, the god of wealth. He indulged himself in all the joys of good living, but none pleased him more than the delights of the table. He imported delicacies and rare spices and herbs from the four corners of the world and sought out the finest chefs, especially those who had had royal patrons.

Soon he was eating like the king himself. At every meal he consumed eighty-four of the most delectable entrees known to man, as well as twelve exquisite sweetmeats, all washed down with the five kinds of beverage. Fortunately, the king did not discover the habits of this usurper of royal privilege.

One day the pandita Bhahana arrived at Dhilipa's house at suppertime and was invited to share the sumptuous banquet. After the meal, however, the pandita spoke to his host of the pain and frustration of the Wheel of Existence and the means of escaping from it. The merchant was so impressed with this discourse that he begged his visitor to remain and become priest to his entire household.

The pandita agreed, and it became his daily custom to lecture to his host while the merchant plied his trade. One day, while watching Dhilipa press the golden oil from the sesame seeds, the guru remarked that while the merchant might well bring in greater and greater profit through such labor, he would certainly not attain liberation.

Dhilipa was deeply struck by this remark. He stopped the press, wiped his hands, and sat down at the feet of his guru. "How then can I acquire liberation, holy one?" he asked.

The pandita's answer was to give him initiation. Then he instructed his disciple in the method of deconditioning his mind from the constructs of the conventional world. The pandita told him that when all thoughts of appearances had dropped from his mind, Dhilipa would see that what remained was naked reality, raw energy, and pure light—the inherent radiance of seemingly concrete objects. And he recited these verses:

> Extract the sesame oil of your body,
> Clarify this liquid as conceptual thought,
> And pour the purified oil
> Into the vessel of mind's empty nature.

> Then, ignite the wick
> Spun from the twin cords of appearance and emptiness
> With the flame of knowledge and pure awareness.

> Thus shall the gloom of ignorance be dispelled,
> And you shall abide for time beyond time
> In the inexhaustible, incomparable pleasure
> Of liberation.

After nine years of meditation, the merchant succeeded in uniting creative and fulfillment meditation. When he attained his goal, a golden radiance began to pour from his being until it illuminated the sky.

When the king heard of this miracle, he sent a messenger to observe the event with his own eyes and report back. Dhilipa sang his reply to the king:

> If wealth is measured by inexhaustible bliss,
> Then I am a king without peer.

People flocked to Dhilipa for instruction, and the wise sage took the measure of each one, as he had measured out his sesame oil. And to each supplicant he gave an instruction that exactly filled the person's nature and abilities. After many years of selfless service, he ascended into the Paradise of the Dakinis with a vast retinue.

DARIKAPA
Slave-King of the Temple Whore

Pure pleasure lies within each of us
But delusion veils it.
Strive as you will for a hundred lifetimes
To acquire virtue and mystical awareness,
You will never realize pure pleasure
Without a guru's guidance.

Late one afternoon, Indrapala, king of Pataliputra, and all his beaters and trackers were returning from hunting a tiger that had been marauding in the countryside. Tired and hungry, the king decided to take the shortest route back to the palace, which led them through the marketplace.

There he spied a crowd of his subjects bowing and giving reverance to someone besides himself. Angered, he rode his mount through the heart of the multitude, where he came face to face with the siddha Luipa. The king recognized him instantly as the yogin renowned for eating only fish entrails that fishermen throw to the dogs when they clean their day's catch.

Indrapala's anger melted away, and he greeted the yogin, whose presence honored his realm. "You are a fine and handsome man," said the king, looking the yogin up and down. "Why don't you give up eating those rotten fish guts? Come to my palace and let me provide you with fine food and all that you require."

Luipa walked around the king, looking him up and down. "Fish guts suit me fine," he said. "And all that I require is release from the wheel of birth and death. Can you give me that?"

"No," said the king. "But if you remain with us I can fulfill your every wish.

203

I will even give you my kingdom if you so desire," he added, testing the yogin.

"Are you offering me the way to deathlessness and eternal youth? That I will accept," Luipa replied.

"All that I can offer you is my kingdom and my daughter's hand in marriage," said the king.

"Bah," said Luipa, shaking his head in disgust. "Of what use are those things to me?"

"Or to me?" said the king, suddenly overwhelmed with revulsion for his own way of life. "Wearing a crown isn't all that much in the great scheme of things. And the wielding of power has many evil repercussions." Whereupon the king rode away deep in thought.

Several days later, the king called his Brahmin minister to him for a private conference. Indrapala confessed that he had been reviewing his life and had come to the startling conclusion that he was not a happy man. The life of luxury, rich food, and fine clothes had not brought him any sense of satisfaction or accomplishment.

"I have decided to abdicate in favor of my son and spend the rest of my life practicing the dharma," said the king.

"It will be my greatest honor to accompany you on this path," replied his faithful minister.

After the new king had been crowned and the reins of government had been turned over to the next administration, the king and his minister, now no better off than the poorest of beggars, made their way to the cremation ground that Luipa was known to frequent. The yogin initiated them both into the mandala of Samvara. However, as neither of them had anything to offer him in return, they agreed to offer him their bodies and become his slaves.

As wandering mendicants, Luipa and the two initiates traveled to Orissa, where they remained for some time practicing their sadhana and begging for food. Then they continued on their journey from town to town, arriving at last in Jantipur, a city of three hundred thousand households.

Jantipur was famed for its great temple, which housed seven hundred dancing girls devoted to the service of the god. Luipa took his slaves with him to the temple, where he sought out Darima, the mistress of the temple whores. But their way was barred by three hundred burly guards protecting the doors to her domain.

In a loud voice Luipa called out, "I have a male slave that may interest your mistress!"

"If I like what I see, I might be interested in buying him," drawled a bored voice from within.

At which the doors of the dancers' chambers opened and out came an extraordinarily beautiful woman with an exquisite figure. The only thing that marred her perfection was a hint of jaded petulance at the corners of her mouth.

Luipa presented the king-turned-slave, and Darima examined him with a practiced eye. Much taken with the prize she was being shown, she offered the siddha the munificent sum of one hundred tolas of gold.

The yogin accepted the offer on two conditions: First, the slave was to have a room to himself and always be able to sleep alone; and second, he was to be released from service as soon as he had earned back his purchase price. Darima agreed, and the bargain was struck.

For twelve years the king served Darima admirably. He washed her feet, massaged her body, saw to the careful preparation of her food, and attended to her every need. But he never once forgot his guru's instruction. He spent every day in service to his mistress, and he spent every night meditating in service to the dharma. The other servants grew to love and respect him for his many kindnesses to them, often performing their tasks for them. In time Darima made him master of her household.

One day, near the end of this period, a very wealthy king by the name of Kunci arrived at the temple with five hundred ounces of gold he had every intention of spending on an orgy of pleasure. The slave-king acted as intermediary for the royal visitor and received seven ounces of gold for every service he provided.

Days and nights of debauchery ensued. Every pleasure was provided, every sense indulged, until even the royal visitor began to be sated. After one particularly lavish feast, Kunci's belly rebelled, and he went out into the night garden to take the air. The night wind was cool and fragrant with a perfume so exquisite the king had to know its source; he intended to take the flowering plant back to his own palace gardens. It was not the familiar jasmine or gardenia intoxicating him, and he began to follow the mysterious scented pathway through the luxuriant foliage to the temple park. In the far distance he spied a faint glow and wondered if the fragrance might be coming from the same source.

As Kunci drew closer, the light became more and more intense, until he stumbled into a small clearing where the radiance dazzled him. Shading his eyes, the king could just make out the form of Darima's slave, seated upon a jeweled throne, attended by fifteen girls of unearthly beauty. He fell back into the shadows, amazed at what he had seen.

As soon as he had his wits about him, Kunci ran back to the temple, calling for Darima. Blindfolding her, he told her to hold tight to his hand, for he had something incredible to show her. She followed, drawn by the heady scent in the air and the intense radiance even through her blindfold.

Freeing her eyes, she gasped in astonishment and fell to her knees before her former slave. Filled with remorse because she had failed to perceive his true nature, she walked round and round his throne, weaving circles in reverent obeisance.

"Forgive me," she said, prostrating herself before the realized yogin. "I am human, and I have made a terrible mistake in not seeing you for the saint you are. I have abused you. I have sinned. Please find it in your heart to pardon me and remain with us as our priest. Allow us to venerate you one year for each year that you have served us."

The slave-king levitated into the sky to the height of seven palm trees and looked down benevolently at the crowd of courtiers, dancing girls, guards, and slaves that had gathered before him. "You are forgiven," he said. "I thank you for your offer, but my service is for all the suffering people of the earth."

Everyone there that night became his disciple, and he gave them instruction on the sadhana known as "emptying the city," singing his verse:

> The fabled riches of kings
> With their canopies, elephants, and thrones
> Pale beside my exalted state.
> For I am shaded by the canopy of liberation,
> Ride the great vehicle of the mahayana,
> And reign on the throne of the three realms—
> This is Darikapa's pleasure!

The master became known from kingdom to kingdom, from continent to continent, as the guru Darikapada, "The Whore's Slave." For many years he served the people selflessly, and when he was assumed bodily into the Paradise of the Dakinis, seven hundred attendants rose with him.

UDHILIPA
The Flying Siddha

Following the meandering course of a thought
Can lead to madness;
Resist, and karma is restrained.
When your home is nowhere
The mind is centered.
There is nothing to be gained
By seeking elsewhere.

In Devikotta there once lived a man of high birth and great wealth. These were the rewards he had accumulated because of his virtue and generosity in previous lives. And he enjoyed his good fortune to the fullest, granting himself and his family every pleasure his imagination could devise.

One day he was drawn to his window because of the patterns of light and shadow playing upon the polished floor. Gazing into the sky he discovered masses of clouds in five colors and an infinite variety of shapes. Here was an elephant with two trunks, there a leopard about to leap, and over there a cat curled up asleep, its tail over its nose. And there, most beautiful of all, was a swan in flight. "What elegance and grace, what power," he thought, "ah, the ecstasy that creature must know!"

He continued to gaze at the swan in his mind's eye long after it had dissolved into a dozen different shapes. The desire to fly began to obsess him. He wished with all his heart and soul to be able to find a way to taste that ultimate pleasure—the thrill of flight.

One day, not long after, the guru Karnaripa (Aryadeva) came to his door to beg food. Udhilipa made him welcome and offered him the best his kitchens

could provide. And then he confessed his deepest desire: Could the yogin teach him to fly?

"Yes," said the guru, "there is a way. But it is long and arduous. Do you think you could attempt such a demanding sadhana?"

"So great is my yearning to take to the sky," replied his host, "that nothing could prevent me from following your instructions."

"Very well then," said Karnaripa, and he gave him the initiation of the Catuspitha-mahayogini Tantra. Then he advised: "Visit the Twenty-Four Great Power Centers. There, you must find out where the Twenty-Four Panaceas, the seed essences of each place, lie hidden. To discover these secrets, you must propitiate the twenty-four dakinis who guard the panaceas by reciting each of their mantras ten thousand times."

Udhilipa set forth on his meditative journey that very day. In time he accomplished the task with which the yogin had charged him. Then he sought out his guru for further instruction.

"You have indeed demonstrated your firm resolve," said Karnaripa. "However, there is an even more difficult task awaiting you."

"Anything, holy one," cried his disciple. "What must I do to learn the secret of flight?"

"Now you must prepare the precious elixir that will enable you to soar with the swans," said the yogin. "The panaceas must be refined to ultimate perfection. This requires three steps: First you must process them in a copper pot, next in a silver pot, and last of all in a pot of pure gold."

Udhilipa's alchemical sadhana took twelve long years. However, in the end he succeeded and gained mahamudra-siddhi. His realization gave him the power to fly effortlessly through the heavens until his entire being was suffused with joy.

His disciples called him The Flying Siddha. After serving humanity selflessly, he flew upon wings of bliss into the Paradise of the Dakinis.

LAKSMINKARA
The Mad Princess

Seekers must first create enlightened vision.
Then they must meditate steadfastly
Upon the emptiness of being.
Lastly, embedded in the intuitive constant
Of the mystical experience,
They do what they must with grace and modesty.

In the dakini realm of Oddiyana, King Indrabhuti ruled the kingdom of Sambhola. To cement the friendly relations between his kingdom and the neighboring one of King Jalendra of Lankapuri, Indrabhuti betrothed his sister Laksminkara at the age of seven to the son of Jalendra. The only thing that divided the two realms in any way was religion, as Sambhola was Buddhist, and Lankapuri was not. However, the two kings did not envision this as a barrier either to friendship or the marriage.

Laksminkara was an extraordinary being. From birth she had been blessed with all the qualities of the elect. She had been delicately brought up, and at an early age the teachings of the guru Kambala and other masters had endowed her with a full understanding of many tantras. Pleading that she was too young to leave home, her family managed to postpone the marriage ceremony until she was sixteen.

Throughout her growing up, that day had always seemed far away to the holy young woman. But at last she had to face the reality of marriage with a prince much older than she, whom she had only seen once nine years before. It felt as though the end of the world had come when the prince's escort arrived to take her away from her home and all that she held dear. After her sheltered upbringing she was terrified of entering the mundane world, when all she wished to do was continue with her practice. Nevertheless, she understood the necessities of diplomacy, and she departed from Sambhola accompanied by a retinue of Buddhist friends and an enormous dowry and sumptuous gifts for her new family.

There had been some delay in her departure, and the royal party arrived some days after they had been expected. They were met outside the gates to King Jalendra's palace by a delegation of court astrologers. They informed her that it was an inauspicious day for her arrival, and she and her retinue must wait where they were until the following day.

Already distressed and uneasy in this new environment, Laksminkara had looked forward to a kind reception. With the delay, she felt she was being very harshly treated and fell into a depression. As she languished outside the palace, observing the life of the city around her, her depression deepened. It was quite clear that the people of this city had never heard the message of the Buddha.

Suddenly, in the distance there was a great clamor of horns and baying dogs and horses' hooves, and then a royal hunting party came galloping past, obviously returning from the chase. At the head of the group rode a stern-faced man in gorgeous clothes soiled by the bloody carcass of a slain doe he had flung across his saddle.

The princess despaired when she witnessed this inhuman treatment of animals. But her hair stood on end and the blood drained from her face when she learned that the prince she had seen was her husband.

"My brother, a prince who cherishes the Buddha's doctrine, has sent me among impious worldlings!" she cried and fainted dead away.

When she revived, she had reached a new resolve. She had all the chests and boxes and bales she had brought with her opened on the spot, and when the curious gathered to stare, she began to give away her entire dowry. Everything went, even her jewelry, which she gave to her attendants before sending them back to Sambhola.

When she was finally allowed into the palace, she locked herself into the chamber her husband had provided and refused to see a single soul for ten days. After much thought, she decided her only escape from this life of torture was to pretend to be insane. And so she tore the clothes from her body, smeared herself with oil and lamp black, unbound her hair and covered it with filth until she looked like a wild woman. But all the while in her heart of hearts she was concentrating fixedly upon her sadhana.

The prince despaired when he saw her. Summoning all the royal physicians, he sent them to examine her. She greeted them with hysterical screams, hurling oil lamps and hairbrushes at their heads, and attacking them with her teeth and fingernails.

A message was sent to her brother, King Indrabhuti, hoping he would intervene. He did nothing, which dismayed the royal family of Lankapuri. They did not understand, as he clearly did, that what his sister was doing was demonstrating her revulsion for samsara. He was ashamed that her spiritual growth so far outstripped his own.

To all appearances, Laksminkara was hopelessly insane. Her behavior had been so erratic that no one wanted to be anywhere near her, which was exactly what she had hoped would happen.

One night, when the guards at her door had gone off to attend to some business of their own, Laksminkara crept out of her room. Like a shadow, she slipped down the back stairways of the labyrinthine palace, eventually finding her way to the empty kitchens. There, she hid among the piles of trash and garbage and escaped through the back gates when the sweepers came to collect the refuse.

She made her way to a cremation ground and, renouncing the world to become a yogini, she lived by scavenging food thrown out for the dogs. A hard path for one so delicately bred, but her determination was unswerving. For seven years she lived in this manner, continually deepening her experience of the essential nirvana until she attained siddhi.

A sweeper of the king's latrines, an untouchable, served her faithfully during this time, and when she gained her realization she gave him initiation. He quickly attained Buddhahood without anyone knowing of his achievement except his preceptress.

Just about this time, King Jalendra, the father of her former fiancé, went out on a royal hunt. He became separated from the rest of the hunting party and, after hours of aimless searching, grew fatigued. He dismounted and fell asleep in the shelter of a tree.

When he awoke it was after nightfall, and he had difficulty finding his way. Leading his horse cautiously through the underbrush, his attention was caught by something in the distance. It seemed to be a light—a very odd occurrence in the middle of the forest. His curiosity aroused, he worked his way closer and closer to the strange glow. Eventually he discovered that it was emanating from the mouth of a cave. He approached quietly and peered inside. There a wondrous sight met his eyes.

Seated upon a jeweled throne was Laksminkara, her body glowing with a golden radiance that suffused the cave with light. She was surrounded by a circle of adoring goddesses. A deep and abiding faith blossomed in the king's heart, and he remained there all night watching the events in the magical cave.

The next day he caught up with the hunting party, which had been searching frantically for him, and they all returned to the city. But King Jalendra could not keep himself from returning to the cave time after time. Finally, one night he could bear the secrecy no longer and he entered the cave and prostrated himself before the yogini.

Not surprisingly, she was quite doubtful about his motives. But the king spoke so movingly of his belief in her as a Buddha, and he begged so humbly for instruction, that in the end she believed in his sincerity and taught him these verses:

All beings on the Wheel of Rebirth suffer,
For in samsara there is not one moment of bliss—
Even superior beings, men and gods, are tormented.

The lower realms are composed of pure pain—
There, ravenous beasts constantly devour each other
And beings are tormented by unending heat and cold.
O king, seek the pure pleasure of release.

"You cannot be my disciple," she continued. "Your guru is one of your very own latrine sweepers. He is one of my disciples who has attained siddhi.

"I have many sweepers," said the king. "How shall I know him?" "Observe them closely," she replied. "Put your trust in the man who feeds the poor after he has finished his work. Go to him at night for instruction." The king did as Laksminkara advised, and it was not long before he discovered the identity of the sweeper-guru. He invited the man to the palace and received him in the throne room. When the sweeper entered, the king rose from his throne, came down the steps, and took the sweeper by the hand. He led the untouchable to his throne and seated him there. And then the king prostrated himself before his guru and requested instruction. The sweeper-yogin gave him initiation by the transfer of the guru's grace, then taught the king the creative and fulfillment stages of the sadhana of Vajra Varahi.

For many years thereafter, Laksminkara and the sweeper performed many miracles in the kingdom of Lankapuri before they both ascended into the Paradise of the Dakinis.

NIRGUNAPA
The Enlightened Moron

Our true guru's precepts show the peaceful center,
Pacifying violent emotions and conflicting thoughts.
Stilling those wavelike disturbances in meditation
We conduct ourselves with attention and poise.

Nirgunapa was born into a family of low-caste householders in Purvadesa. His birth was attended by a great feast and celebration. But as he grew up, unable to perform even the simplest tasks, his parents became disillusioned. Their son was stricken by a moronic lassitude.

"This moron can do neither good nor bad," his family would say. "It would have been better had he not been born."

One day, unspeakably depressed after being reviled in this way, Nirgunapa moped off and laid himself down in a lonely place, where a yogin found him. "Get up and beg alms in town," the yogin told him.

"I can't get up," Nirgunapa replied, unwilling to stir.

Out of pity the yogin gave him food. "Do you have any skill?" he inquired.

"Venerable sir, my name is Moron," he said as a matter of fact. "I have no skill whatsoever."

"But you need to eat and drink," insisted the yogin. "Aren't you afraid of death?"

"Yes, surely," Nirgunapa admitted. "But what can I do?"

"I will give you a sadhana, if you can practice it," the yogin offered.

"If I can practice it lying down, please teach me," Nirgunapa responded.

The yogin initiated him and instructed him in the indivisibility of appearances and emptiness:

Both "the knower" and "the known" are delusory,
And those who fail to realize this
Suffer hopeless anxiety and should be pitied.
Yet even this anxiety has no basis in reality.
When the mindstream has become clear light—
The indivisibility of appearances and emptiness—
Free of inhibition, you can wander
In the villages as a crazy saint.

Nirgunapa followed these instructions, begging his food and practicing his sadhana, until he realized the unity of appearances and emptiness as clear light and attained his goal. People who met him in his wanderings would ask him who he was, whereupon he would gaze into their eyes and weep; seeing the depth of compassion in his heart, they would weep with him. Those who were fit vessels he made his disciples, teaching them that form is emptiness and emptiness is form. Gradually, their delusions dissolved like a boat sinking into the ocean, and they attained mahamudra-siddhi. Nirgunapa was assumed bodily into the Paradise of the Dakinis.

MEKHALA and KANAKHALA
The Headless Sisters

When all inner and outer phenomena
Are perceived as mind,
All things have the same flavor.
In supreme effortless meditation
I found nondual pleasure—pure and perfect Buddhahood.

Donning the impregnable armor of patience
Crowned with diamond-like fortitude,
I embarked in the vessel of my mind
And confidently took possession of my body.

An elderly widower of Devikotta found himself burdened with two unmarried daughters. This, in itself, wasn't so bad. But the two girls had been infamous since birth for their impish natures and mischievous tricks. They were always up to something, and what one didn't think up, the other did.

Their father was lucky to marry them off to the unsuspecting sons of a fisherman in another village. However, it wasn't long before the bridegrooms realized their mistake. The sisters made their lives miserable, and they in turn never stopped criticizing their wives' behavior. To make matters worse, the neighbors gossiped about them all with acid tongues.

Despite the fact that they were the authors of their own misery, the two young women complained to each other about the hardness of their lot day and night. Finally, the younger one suggested that they run away.

"I can't stand this life another minute," Kanakhala complained. "Why don't we go to another country and see if things are any better there?"

But Mekhala, for once in her life, spoke wisely to her sister. "You know," she said thoughtfully, "I suspect that we deserve what we get. We bring it on ourselves. I hate to tell you this, but we're going to have to stay—it isn't going to be different anywhere else because we take ourselves with us."

At that very moment the most amazing rumpus erupted outside in the street. The two young women ran out just in time to see the guru Krsnacarya pass by with seven hundred dakas and dakinis in attendance. A canopy floated magically in the air over his head, and numerous *damaru* skull drums sounded in the sky around him.

Impulsively, the sisters threw themselves at his feet, confessed their entire unhappy story, and begged for his instruction.

Whereupon Krsna gave them initiation and instructed them in the Vajra Varahi path that unites vision and action. Then he sent them away to practice their sadhana.

The two sisters meditated diligently for twelve years and successfully attained their goal. Awakening to the world once more, they decided to travel together to visit their guru and seek further instruction. They found him in his hermitage and humbly prostrated themselves before him, then walked about him in reverential circles.

The guru received them kindly, but it was quite obvious that he had no idea who they were.

The sisters were very disappointed. "Don't you remember us?" they asked, "We're the two unhappily married sisters you initiated twelve years ago."

"If I gave you initiation," replied the guru angrily, "then why haven't you brought me any offerings!"

"We are at your service," replied the sisters. "Tell us what you would like."

"Your heads!" he demanded without a moment's thought.

"We give what the guru asks," they replied without a moment's hesitation. Each of the sisters reached down her throat and pulled out the keenedged sword of pure awareness. In the blink of an eye they decapitated themselves and as they made their offering to their guru, the severed heads sang:

> Through the grace of the guru's instruction
> We have blended creative and fulfillment meditation.
> We have destroyed all distinction between samsara and nirvana.

We have united vision and action in perfect harmony.
We know no distinction between acceptance and rejection.

Dwelling in the blessed unity of vast space and pure awareness,
We know no separation between self and others.
As tokens of achieving the indeterminate state
We offer these gifts.

In great delight the guru exclaimed:

Behold these two great yoginis—
They have reached their goal in joy!
And now, forget your own peace and happiness,
Begin to live for the sake of others.

Whereupon Krsnacarya replaced each head so perfectly on its own shoulders that no scar or blemish remained to tell the tale of their experience. The assembled people were amazed and awed, and ever after the sisters were known as the Headless Yoginis.

In gratitude Mekhala and Kanakhala knelt before their guru and touched his feet in reverence. No sooner had they done so than they attained mahamudra-siddhi. For many years thereafter they worked selflessly for the benefit of all sentient beings and were assumed bodily into the Paradise of the Dakinis.

KIRAPALAPA (KILAPA)
The Repentant Conqueror

As a cloud blocks the light of the sun
I was blocked from the light of reality
By my concepts of self and other.
But, at the moment of my realization,
My mind basked in the radiance
Of its own emptiness.
Even Buddha became a meaningless label.

The king of Grahara was a restless man who was never satisfied with what he had. Contentment eluded him like a never-ending dream.

Although he ruled a vast and prosperous kingdom and enjoyed pleasures as varied and magnificent as Kubera, the god of wealth himself, it was never enough. He was ever grasping at more territory, more riches. To satisfy his hunger, his armies were always warring with the neighboring kingdoms, and they were always victorious.

One day, hungering for glory as well as empire, the king accompanied one of his forces on a plundering mission to the capital city of a distant kingdom. This success would push his borders to the sea, and who knew what wealth untold would then be his.

While he had trained at arms since he was a boy, he had never before witnessed the horrors of war with his own eyes. With growing revulsion he watched as his own men butchered old men and women too helpless to move out of the way. He saw infants snatched from their mothers and smashed against walls like clay pots; young women handed like chattel from one soldier to the next to do with as they pleased. He saw wives left without husbands, children without

223

mothers, everyone without homes. The king's nostrils were filled with the smell of blood, his ears with screams, his eyes with horror, and his heart with the knowledge that he was the author of all this needless misery.

He underwent a complete transformation and became profoundly repentant. Compassion welled up within him, and he withdrew his army beyond the walls of the city. There he did what he could to make amends for what he had inflicted upon these people. He ordered the city rebuilt, restored families to each other, cared for widows and orphans, wrote a treaty of peace.

When he returned home to his own city, he was determined to embark upon a new way of life. He rang the great bell of charity and distributed all of his immense fortune to the poor.

Just about this time, a tattered yogin came to the palace gates begging food. The king invited him to his own table and offered him the best he had. After they had eaten, the king told the yogin about his great change of heart and his desire to practice a sadhana. The yogin taught him how to take refuge in the Triple Gem and how to practice the Bodhisattva Vow and the Four Boundless States of Mind. But, true to his own nature, the king was not satisfied with this. He begged the yogin to teach him the dharma that leads to Buddhahood in a single lifetime. The yogin warned him of the difficulties of this path, but the king was adamant. Whereupon the yogin gave him the Samvara initiation and empowerment, and he instructed the king on creative fulfillment meditation.

With great determination, the king set out upon the path. But before very long he began to experience the very difficulties of which he had been warned. He had spent a lifetime preoccupied with the affairs of government and the army. Every time he tried to meditate, his thoughts would return time and again to his old preoccupations. Once more he consulted his guru. This time the yogin devised a sadhana that used these very thoughts as stepping-stones on a path of self-liberation:

> Visualize all beings of the three realms
> As a host of proud warriors.
> Unite them into one disciplined force—
> The infinite emptiness of mind—
> And see all your enemies defeated.
> Then, Great King, bask in the bliss
> Of victory.

For twelve years King Kirapalapa meditated in this fashion, gaining enlightenment and siddhi. On the day of his realization, his body began to emit a golden glow that soon engulfed his entire palace. As the radiance flowed through the palace like the rays of the rising sun, all the king's wives and ministers understood that he had achieved his goal, and they gathered before him to pay him homage. This was the instruction that he gave them:

> Transform the lust for power and riches
> Into the desire to relate to all beings
> In the four boundless states of mind.
> With the keen edge of your warrior's rage,
> Destroy every demon that enters your mind.

After seven hundred years of selfless service to all sentient beings, the king ascended into the Paradise of the Dakinis with six hundred disciples.

NAGABODHI
The Red-Horned Thief

What good fortune to live upon the earth.
What riches are held in the ocean's depths.
What pleasure in wielding the sword of awareness
And meeting friends when we encounter the Aim-less Ones.

༄

Many years ago Arya Nagarjuna was residing at the Suvarna Vihara. Every night a feast was provided for him and served upon plates of purest gold. One evening as he sat down to his elegant dinner, a Brahmin from western India chanced to pass his door and peer in. However, it was more than mere curiosity that stopped the man in his tracks when he saw the gleaming golden service. For he had become a thief, and the sight of so much gold dazzled him and excited his greed.

Yet before he could even begin to devise a plan to steal the treasure, a golden chalice came flying out the door and landed in his hands. Astounded at his luck, and not caring to question it further, he tucked the chalice in his robes and beat a hasty retreat.

The following night he passed by Nagarjuna's door again. As the thief tried to decide the best way to get into the house unnoticed, a golden platter came sailing out the window like some great gilded bird and caught him on the shin. Dumbfounded, the thief again tucked his treasure in his robes and limped into the twilight.

Figuring the third time is always the luckiest, the thief came again the following night, planning to make off with the entire cache. But no sooner had he approached the corner of the house and was edging toward the open door than all the remaining plates, bowls, and cups came racketing out the door and piled themselves up neatly at his feet. This time the thief was frozen in his tracks, never before in his experience of the world had such a thing happened. Who was living here? Was that person reading his mind?

"My wealth is yours," called a friendly voice from inside the house. "No need to steal anything. Come in. Eat and drink with me. My name is Arya Nagarjuna. Stay as long as you like, and when you're ready to leave take whatever you want."

Utterly astonished, the thief entered the house and had supper with the saint. He had never met anyone like this, and he wanted to test out this strange being. Nagarjuna's conversation settled all the thief's doubts and awakened his faith and implicit trust in the guru.

In the end all he wished to take away with him was the guru's golden instruction. Nagarjuna was delighted and initiated the thief into the Guhya-samaja Tantra. Then he gave him instruction on how to meditate upon greed and find the path to self-liberation:

> First, abandon all thought of action.
> Then, at the fontanel on the crown of your head,
> Visualize a large horn, translucent and red,
> Radiating a ruby light.
> This is the horn of desirable objects—
> See them as mere concepts, delusory mental pictures.

Nagarjuna then filled the thief's hut with diamonds, rubies, sapphires, pearls, emeralds, and opals—every imaginable treasure was here. And the thief, content beyond measure, sat down to meditate on the guru's instructions.

Twelve years passed. An enormous horn grew out of the top of his skull, and it pulsed with an angry red light as though it were a living thing. His body was convulsed and shuddering. The poor thief was in torment.

When Nagarjuna appeared to him and asked him how he fared, his pupil described terrible suffering. The master immediately understood his problem and gave him further instruction:

> This great horn, built cell by cell
> From appearances and fixed notions,
> Is destroying your happiness,
> For attachment to seemingly concrete objects
> Is always a cause for suffering.

But these objects of desire
Have no real existence.
Events have no more reality
Than clouds swirling through the sky.
How then can birth, life, or death
Harm or profit us in any way?

When both the knower and that which is known
Are essentially emptiness,
How can the pure nature of mind
Be affected in any way at all.

Through Nagarjuna's words, Nagabodhi came to realize the emptiness of the nature of his being. Deeply absorbed in this awareness, within six months his red horn had completely disappeared, and he realized the indivisibility of samsara and nirvana. He attained his goal of liberation.

When the time came for Nagarjuna's departure from the earth plane, he summoned Nagabodhi and appointed him his successor and master of the lineage he had founded. Nagarjuna then empowered the realized thief to give his disciples the Eight Great Siddhis when the appropriate time arose.

These magical powers conferred on the realized one the ability to pass through earth and rock; to wield the sword of awareness; to destroy and annihilate; to create and enrich; to dispense the pill of divine vision; to apply the eye salve of omniscience; the ability to walk at blinding speeds; and the secret of the alchemy of eternal life.

Nagarjuna then commanded Nagabodhi to remain on Sri Parvata Mountain to work selflessly for all sentient beings until he received the revelation of the arrival of the Maitreya, the Buddha Yet to Come, who would dispense loving-kindness throughout the four corners of the world.

It is said that he will remain there for twenty thousand years.

SARVABHAKSA
The Empty-Bellied Siddha

In ignorance, different flavors are distinct;
In realization, all flavors are essentially one.
In ignorance, samsara and nirvana are separate;
In realization, they are the union of pure pleasure.

Sarvabhaksa was a man of low caste and enormous appetite. He was born hungry. He spent his days trying to fill his huge belly. He went to sleep hungry. He dreamed of food all night. And he awoke hungry all over again. He would eat anything and everything—but it was never enough.

One day his driving appetite overreached his ability to fill it. There simply wasn't enough food to satisfy his terrible craving. In utter despair he retreated to a cave to bemoan his obsession with food and his aching belly.

The guru Saraha found him there and asked what was wrong, why was he weeping and groaning in such distress?

"There's a fire raging in my gut, holy one," said the glutton. "It consumes everything. I can never satisfy it. Today I didn't find enough to eat, and I'm in terrible pain."

"If you can't endure so small a hunger as this," asked the guru, "what will you do when you're reborn as a hungry ghost?"

"A hungry ghost?" cried Sarvabhaska in horror. "What is that?"

Saraha lifted the veil from the pupil's eyes just long enough to point out one of the wretched wraiths. "Their karma of greed and avarice dooms them to ten thousand years of endless agony," he warned. "Their mouths are like the eye of a needle, their throats are thin as a hair, and their stomachs are like empty mountains. They are suffering endless desire for food, and they are forbidden the slightest satisfaction."

The glutton was shaken to the roots of his being. He prostrated himself before Saraha and begged, "How can I save myself from such a horrible fate? Please teach me the way to release."

Saraha knew that the only cure for such a fate was compassion and generosity, and so he initiated his disciple into the path of Bhusuku, who was known as "the embodiment of indolence":

> Visualize your belly as the empty sky;
> In food and drink see all phenomena;
> Feel your digestive heat as the final conflagration;
> When you eat, consume the universe.

The glutton practiced this meditation with great devotion. So enormous was his appetite in sadhana, he ate every last stone of Mount Meru. Even this was not enough. In consuming the universe, he swallowed the sun and the moon. The land was deprived of all light, and the people were terrified.

The dakinis searched high and low until they found the guru Saraha and begged him for help. The yogin returned to his meditating pupil and gave him this further advice: "Visualize everything you eat as absolute nothingness."

With this instruction the glutton was able to understand the identical nature of appearances and emptiness, and thus he attained his goal. The sun reappeared to illuminate the day, and the moon shone her silver light as a blessing in the darkness of night. The people rejoiced.

After fifteen years of practice Sarvabhaksa attained mahamudra-siddhi. For six hundred years thereafter he served humanity with compassion and generosity. Accompanied by a thousand disciples he entered the Paradise of the Dakinis.

MANIBHADRA
The Model Wife

When my mind was shrouded in ignorance,
Critical thought attended every sound.
But when my mind's nature was revealed to me,
I understood that whatever appeared before me
Was reality itself.

In the town of Agarce many years ago there lived a wealthy householder with a beautiful thirteen-year-old daughter. As was the custom, she was betrothed at that age to a man of her own caste, but she was allowed to continue living at home until she was old enough to take up her wifely duties.

Manibhadra chanced to be in her mother's kitchen one afternoon when the guru Kukkuripa came to her house begging food. She welcomed him and served him with her own hands, all the while peeping shyly at him under lowered lashes.

Finally, throwing girlish modesty to the winds, she exclaimed, "What a handsome man you are! Why do you go about in patched robes begging for food, when you could take a wife and live as comfortably as my father?"

The yogin laughed with delight at the girl's innocent inquiry. "Thank you, my dear," he said, "but that is exactly what I am trying to avoid. I'm terrified of the wheel of rebirth, and I live this way and practice meditation because I'm trying to free myself from the karmic round of life after life. I may not get another chance anytime soon, you know."

"Why is that, holy sir?" asked the girl, wide-eyed with interest.

"That is because human birth is a precious opportunity to make spiritual progress," he replied. "When I realized that, I gave up my old life and all thoughts of women."

Manibhadra's faith was immediately kindled, and such was her trust of the yogin that she begged him to show her the way to liberation.

"I live in the cremation ground. Everyone knows me," replied Kukkuripa. "If you want to know more, just ask for me there." Then he thanked her for her hospitality and departed.

Manibhadra was so lost in thought over what the yogin had said to her, that she neglected her chores for the rest of the day. When night came she could not sleep, so eager was she to learn more. So she rose, dressed, and slipped unnoticed out of the sleeping household.

Although she had never been out alone in her life, she walked fearlessly through the shadowy streets to the cremation ground. A kind beggar showed her the way to Kukkuripa's hut, and the yogin welcomed her in.

Recognizing the maturity of her mind and the sincerity of her purpose, the yogin gave his young supplicant initiation and empowerment. Then he instructed her in the practice of creative and fulfillment meditation. Kukkuripa allowed the girl to remain in his hut alone for seven days while she established herself in the practice of her sadhana.

However, when she was nowhere to be found, her family grew frantic with worry. They didn't know what could possibly have happened to their daughter or where to turn. Here they were, one of the finest families in town—a pure bloodline going back for generations—such a blot on their reputation had never occurred before. They didn't know whether to weep with grief or shame.

When Manibhadra finally returned, her parents beat her and called her every sort of name for disappearing and causing such a scandal. It was amazing that her betrothed was still willing to honor their engagement.

With great calm and presence, their daughter defended herself. "There is no one in the universe who has not been either a father or a mother to me," she said. "After all, why was I born into a family with a pure bloodline and fine reputation if such good fortune doesn't allow me to free myself from the grip of samsara. I have been with my guru, who has taught me how to practice a sadhana of liberation. And I have already begun."

Manibhadra's parents were so impressed with their daughter's bearing and assurance that they could find no words to answer her. And they raised no objections when she asked to be relieved of her household duties in order to practice her sadhana one-pointedly.

A year passed. And the time grew near for Manibhadra's fiancé to claim his bride. The family was filled with anxiety, certain she would refuse to fulfill her obligation. Imagine their surprise when she accompanied her husband to her new home with no complaint and no resistance.

Her family was even more astonished when they heard that Manibhadra had become a model wife. She did all and more than was expected of her with great cheerfulness and affection. She never lost her temper and always spoke sweetly and behaved modestly. In good time she gave birth to a son and then a daughter and brought them up in an exemplary manner. Hers was the happiest of households.

In this fashion twelve years passed in perfect harmony. Early one morning, the thirteenth anniversary of meeting with her guru, as luck would have it, she was on her way back from the stream, carrying a pitcher of water on her head. Deep in meditation, she failed to notice a tree root that had freed itself from the earthen path. She tripped and fell, and the pitcher crashed to the ground and broke.

No one saw her for the rest of the day. They searched high and low, and then late in the afternoon someone remembered that she had gone out earlier for water. Her anxious husband went looking for her and found her sitting quietly in the middle of the path, gazing fixedly at the broken bits of pitcher.

He spoke to her, but she seemed totally unaware of his presence. He tried shouting at her, and then he attempted to lift her from the ground, but she remained utterly rooted to the spot. He called the neighbors to see if they could do anything.

But Manibhadra remained immobile and silent until nightfall. Then she looked up, surprised to see such a gathering around her. Her eyes clear and shining, she looked at them all tenderly and sang this song of realization:

> From the beginning of time, sentient beings
> Have broken their vessels, and their lives end.
> But why do they then return home?
> Today, I have broken my vessel.
> But I am abandoning my samsara home
> For the realms of pure pleasure.

How wonderful is the guru—
If you desire happiness, rely on him.

So saying, Manibhadra levitated into the sky and remained there for twenty-one days, giving instruction to the people of Agarce. And then she bid farewell to her family and neighbors and was assumed bodily into the Paradise of the Dakinis.

SARORUHA
The Lotus Child

Overpowered in the great power place of Tathata,
Basuka, the Naga King of Knowledge
Showered gijis upon the suffering people.
When propitiated, the Naga King
Showers knowledge of the tantric mysteries
Upon male and female initiates.

Although Indrabhuti, King of Kanci, ruled over 1,400,000 households, he still had no son and heir. This was a great cause of sadness for the king and his wife, and a cause of great worry for his people, who could see this reign of peace and prosperity ending in a great war of succession.

The king prayed night and day, invoking both worldly and heavenly gods to bring him a son. Such was his merit that in time it became clear that a being had indeed entered his wife's womb. It was an easy, joyous pregnancy, and with the passing of each month, the queen became increasingly tranquil.

Late in her sixth month, the queen had a series of three dreams. First, she dreamed that she ate Mount Meru. In the second she drank the ocean dry; and in the third she suppressed the three realms with the sole of her foot. When she recounted these strange dreams to her husband, he was as puzzled as she, and he called in the palace priests and astrologers to interpret them. But they too were puzzled and unable to agree among themselves what the dreams might portend.

Finally, the king offered a great reward to anyone who could interpret the queen's dreams. A great gathering convened, and the consensus of their wisdom was that the dreams were signs that a Bodhisattva who would rule over the

Kingdom of Truth would be born to the king and queen. Their worldly subjects would be displeased, as there would be no resolution of the succession question. However, there would be signs at the hour of his birth that would ease their minds.

At midnight, on the tenth night of the ninth month after his conception, the child was born. But the birth was very mysterious. Because of the infant's previous karma and merit, he emerged from the pollen bed at the heart of a magnificent lotus in the center of a lake. And at the moment of his birth a shower of riches rained down upon all the inhabitants of the kingdom.

Delighted by their sudden wealth, the people wondered at the cause of such great good fortune, and they began to search for signs of a miraculous occurrence. At noon on the following day, a fisherman discovered the lotus-born child floating in his flower crib in the center of the lake, and with great rejoicing he was borne to the palace.

Within a year the queen had given birth to another son. It was he who ruled in his brother's place when the elder son claimed his lotus-born heritage, renounced the throne, and became a monk. To further his spiritual education, the young monk decided to journey to the great stupa of Sri Dhanyakataka, where the Buddha himself taught the Kalacakra Tantra.

On the journey he chanced to meet another monk heading for the same destination, and they decided to travel together. In actuality the older monk was none other than the Bodhisattva of Compassion, Avalokitesvara, the guru of the lotus-born king. He tested his young companion's honesty and sure-rootedness upon the spiritual path, then offered to instruct him in the Buddha's mode of consummate enjoyment, the sambhogakaya.

The young monk was eager for this teaching, but Avalokitesvara insisted that he first demonstrate his faith and devotion to his guru by admitting that he was unable to manifest the sambhogakaya without his teacher's assistance. Saroruha prostrated himself before the Bodhisattva, who then revealed the reality of Hevajra and his retinue. The young initiate recognized the identity of his guru when he vanished into thin air after instructing his disciple.

Saroruha continued on to Sri Dhanyakataka to begin practicing the sadhana that would allow him to realize all that had been revealed to him in his initiation. Not long after he arrived, a man who looked like a yogin offered to be his servant throughout the years of meditation if the royal monk would consent to initiate him when Saroruha attained siddhi himself. The bargain was struck, and the disciple moved into an empty cave near his master and tended his every need for twelve years.

Unknown to the royal monk, when he began his own retreat so did the rains of the blessed monsoon. Drought struck the land a staggering blow. Each year, the crops were poorer and poorer until the new sprouts simply withered in the blistering heat. The specter of famine was everywhere, carrying off the very old and the very young. All who remained were starving.

Saroruha's servant was afraid to tell his master of the great evil stalking the land for fear that he would abandon his meditation and thus postpone his servant's initiation. The yogin found such food as he could and subsisted off the master's leavings. However, by the end of the twelve years there was no food to be had anywhere. The royal granaries had been opened, and meager rations of rice were being doled out to the populace. The servant went to the palace to beg food and was given a bowl of uncooked rice.

Very, very carefully, minding each precious grain, the servant carried the treasure back to his master's cave. But just as he crossed the threshhold his own strength failed, and he collapsed. The grains of rice scattered across the floor of the cave.

"Are you drunk?" asked his guru, annoyed at the fuss.

"No, Master," replied the faithful servant, "where could I possibly find liquor?" Then, unable to hide the truth any longer, he confessed the truth: "I am weak from hunger."

"Why haven't you eaten?" asked Saroruha, surprised. And the rest of the story came tumbling out.

"Why didn't you tell me!" thundered the monk in a towering rage. "I have the power to make the rains come and the grain grow. Leave me!"

Saroruha then gathered up every grain of the spilled rice and carried them to a nearby stream. There he made offerings of sacramental cakes to the Eight Great Naga guardians. With mudra, mantra, and samadhi, he tortured the Naga Kings until their heads nearly burst from the racket and they appeared before him and acknowledged his mastery over them.

"This famine is your doing," said the master reproachfully. "The deaths of all these innocent people are on your heads. And you will now make amends for your outrageous behavior. Today you will send a shower of rice that fills every starving stomach in the drought-ridden land. Tomorrow you will send a shower of grain. The next day you will send a shower of every sort of provision.

And the three days after that you will send showers of gold and jewels. On the seventh day—SEND RAIN!"

The Eight Naga Kings obeyed this difficult command to the letter. For six days abundance poured down upon the starving people, and their suffering was alleviated. On the seventh day the rains came and the cycle of life began once more. The thirsty earth drank deep, and overnight a fine haze of green blanketed the fields. Withered trees put forth new leaves, and grasses grew in abundance to feed the survivors of the flocks and herds. In due course wombs again carried life, and a fine crop of infants—human and animal—brought joy to every household.

Searching out the source of the miracles, the people soon recognized the master's power. And as more and more people learned of him, their faith was wakened.

Eventually Saroruha forgave his servant's error and granted him initiation and empowerment. He then instructed his disciple, whose name was Rama, in the creative and fulfillment meditation of Hevajra but added this warning: "If you fail to act selflessly for the sake of others, you will never attain the Paradise of the Dakinis. Go now to Sri Parvata Mountain and practice your sadhana there."

So saying, the master floated into the sky and disappeared from sight.

Rama went to Sri Parvata, where he won a beautiful princess for his consort. The pair went on retreat into the jungle, where they built a temple to the god Rama and practiced their sadhana faithfully until they were assumed bodily into the Paradise of the Dakinis.

PUBLISHER'S NOTE

This book has been a labor of love many times in the making. The stories, lessons, and artwork are timeless representations of the human experience.

We would like to express our appreciation to the following people for their diligent and patient work on this book:

Kendra Crossen, Bruce Benderson, Barbara Shor, Norman Kanter, Irving Perkins Associates, Brian Boland, Pamela Bloom, Vince Beck, and Inner Traditions staff members Leslie Colket, Susan Davidson, Jon Desautels, and Meghan MacLean.

Our thanks go as well to the siddhas, who have seen fit to test our determination during our many efforts to keep their legends alive.

EHUD C. SPERLING